Max Walker is a footballer, cricketer, sporting commentator, raconteur, motivational speaker and best-selling author of *How to Hypnotise Chooks*, *How to Tame Lions*, *How to Kiss a Crocodile*, *How to Puzzle a Python*, *The Best of Mr Walker*, *A Chip Off the Old Block*, and the CD-ROM *All Stitched Up*.

Brian Doyle is a writer, actor and stand-up comic. He has worked in television and radio as a writer and performer. In a lifetime of jokes and joking, Brian has won five MO awards and the Golden Stylus for radio commercials. He has appeared on 'IMT', the 'Rugby League Show', the 'Big Gig' and the 'Midday Show'.

MAX WALKER & BRIAN DOYLE

SPORTS jokes

A Sue Hines Book

Allen & Unwin

DISCLAIMER

Australians love a good joke . . . where would a day be without a new laugh?

To all who enjoy the retelling of a yarn, creating the funny line . . . or just sharing the want to laugh . . . thank you for the stimulus to construct this wedge of paper.

MW & BD

First published in 1997
A Sue Hines Book
Allen & Unwin Pty Ltd
9 Atchison Street
St Leonards, NSW 2065 Australia
Phone: (61 2) 9901 4088
Fax: (61 2) 9906 2218
E-mail: frontdesk@allen-unwin.com.au
URL: http://www.allen-unwin.com.au

National Library of Australia
Cataloguing-in-Publication data:
Walker, Max, 1948–
    Sports jokes.
    ISBN 1 86448 512 4.
    1. Australian wit and humor. 2. Sports – Humor. I. Doyle, Brian C.
    (Brian Christopher). II. Title.
796.640994

Designed and typeset by P.A.G.E. Pty Ltd
Cover caricature by Paul Harvey
Printed by Griffin Press

10 9 8 7 6 5 4 3 2 1

To Isabella Kate Walker, who was born on the day this collection of sports laughs was completed: 17 May 1997.

And to Rowena Sheridan Doyle, who made sure this book would be completed on time. A reason to smile.

Contents

Cricket

★For a long time we dreamed of a real leather ball, and at last my brother had one for his birthday. The feel of the leather, the stitching round it, the faint gold letters stamped upon it, the touch of the seam, the smell of it, all affected me so deeply that I still have that ache of beauty when I hold a cricket ball.

—Alison Uttley

★ I was both lucky and privileged to bat in the same line-up as the person 50 per cent responsible for my creation. So as captain of a team named the Liquor Trades it seemed only right that Max Walker senior bat at No. 1 and Max Walker junior bat at No. 2. We also played several district matches together in the North Hobart B-grade side. Whichever way you looked, we were very distinguishable: he was the slow one. He shaved. And he was the one with the rather large 'verandah over the tool shed'.

As you may have guessed, this was no ordinary cricket team. Characters that perhaps would be more at home in a circus turned up most Wednesday mornings to play in a 21-over competition against the Cabbies, Wharfies, the Army, Tramways, Prison Warders—on one occasion, even the 'gaolbirds' themselves were freed for some serious 'R 'n' R'.

Dress rules for playing were slack. The majority walked onto the paddock wearing exactly the clobber they arrived in.

Big Max cut a wholesome silhouette as he ambled

from the darkness of the dressing sheds through the doorway towards the boundary line—keys jingling a xylophonic tune, both hands thumbing his braces as he adjusted his eyes to the bright sunlight.

He always wore firemen's or police braces on match days. No matter how firmly my mother would sew on his buttons, they kept breaking away. Being a skilled carpenter and joiner, he inserted 1½ inch galvanised nails gently in and out of folds in both the front and back of the trousers at waist height. The leather bracer hole was then threaded over the nail— true to its name, firmly braced. Six nails were needed to complete the exercise—and, being galvanised, they didn't rust against a sweaty belly.

★ As the batsman passed the man in the white coat, he said, 'That was never an LBW—you need glasses.'

And the man in the white coat replied, 'So do you mate, I'm selling ice-cream.'

★ Dennis Lillee and Jeff Thomson were a fearsome combination, both on and off the green. An interviewer once said to Lillee, 'Tell me, Dennis, what would you do if you discovered you only had 30 minutes to live?'

Dennis said 'I'd make love to the first thing that moved.'

'And what would you do Mr Thomson?' and Thommo said, 'I wouldn't move for half an hour.'

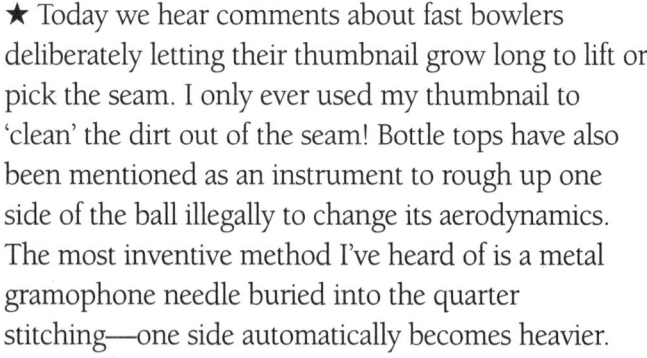

★ Today we hear comments about fast bowlers deliberately letting their thumbnail grow long to lift or pick the seam. I only ever used my thumbnail to 'clean' the dirt out of the seam! Bottle tops have also been mentioned as an instrument to rough up one side of the ball illegally to change its aerodynamics. The most inventive method I've heard of is a metal gramophone needle buried into the quarter stitching—one side automatically becomes heavier.

Then there's the pocketful of dirt, a healthy layer of Vaseline in the fob pocket . . . some bowlers have even used talcum powder to maintain a shine on the ball.

Big Max used to gain much delight from using part of his uniform to lift the seam of a two-piece leather ball, occasionally to the point of the ridiculous. Depending on exactly where and how 'alert' the honorary umpires were, his permanent left or right battery of galvanised 1 1/2 inch nails was available.

★ Do you realise if identical twins Steve and Mark Waugh married identical twin sisters it would only be a matter of time before they were accused of wife swapping?

★ I once asked Steve Waugh if he and his brother were identical twins. He said, 'I am but he's not.'

★ I wonder if Mark Waugh ever forgets Steve Waugh's birthday?

★ Mark Waugh used to be nicknamed Afghanistan . . . the forgotten war—but not any more!

★ One memorable Hobart day, when the wind was blowing a gale straight up the Derwent River all the way from Antarctica, the bails kept blowing off. Big Max generously offered to hammer two of his precious galvanised stakes into the heart of the timber bails—end to end. Being heavier they stayed anchored to the top of the stumps. Also exceptionally handy for removing splinters, cleaning mud off soles of boots, marking the batting crease, even cleaning an umpire's 'Briar' pipe stem or flaking the cheats' tobacco!

Never upset an umpire, particularly on a cold day—because they will never take their hand out of their pocket. 'Umpire with two holes in pocket leave no stone unturned' . . . I think that may have been Confucius.

★ The British tabloid press has a terrible reputation, perhaps best illustrated when the Australian cricket team made a visit to the London Zoo.

A young boy fell into the bear pit and was being mauled by two bears. Without hesitation two of the Australian cricketers jumped into the pit and grappled with the bear until he released the boy.

The next day's headlines: 'Aussie cricketers beat up dumb animal.'

★ 'Wicket keepers,' says Pat, 'are all the same in one way. There is no two of them alike.'

★ My wife is really silly, last week she said I treat cricket as a religion.

I told her not to be so silly. But if she wanted to discuss it could she please wait until the Reverend Benaud and Father Bill Lawry had finished speaking.

★ The classic radio story of a batsman hit by a rising ball just below the belt buckle: he fell to the ground in agony, and as he rose most unsteadily to his feet the commentator said, 'I think he's going to finish the over. He's only got one ball left.'

★ Mop bucket story

There was one night in the north of England in 1975 when some of our Test heroes were having a quiet one that we will never forget. The local watering hole had a beaut, intimate atmosphere—low ceilings, dim lighting, great for a social night out.

Those terrors of the 1975 Ashes tour—West Australians Dennis Lillee and Rodney Marsh—were there having a quiet sip from their Whitbread 'pint' mugs between bets.

I should tell you that in England you're in no danger at all of getting a cold beer . . . well, in those days we weren't . . . because they didn't even store the beer close to the fridge, let alone inside it. So there they were—Rodney and Dennis, pint mugs in hand, with tons of ice blocks melting as quickly as they could get them into the warm beer.

Down went the pints—one, two, three, four, five. About half an hour later, nature took its course. That fabled drinker, Rodney Marsh, was the first to signal to the little Pommie barman. 'Hey pal, whereabouts is the GENTS?' he demanded. Bacchus chuckled at the directions shouted across the bar: 'Down the corridor, over the dirt track, come to the green saw-tooth door . . . and that's it!'

'Bloody beauty, we're away . . . ' Rodney says, as he sways to his feet. Five steps forward and three back, the little fat fella waddled out of the bar, bounced off the walls of the corridor and across the dirt track until he spied a green saw-tooth door.

'Aaah!' Very few sensations in the world even go close to that when you're under pressure, do they?

About fifteen minutes and a few more pints Lillee realised his drinking partner still hadn't returned. Must have fallen in, the fast bowler chuckled. So across the bar . . . down the corridor . . . over the dirt track—not much quicker or straighter than Marshie had managed—marched Dennis. He came to the same green saw-tooth door and barked his arrival.

'Hey, Bacchus! Bacchus, what's happened? You fallen in or something?'

A pained reply came under door. 'No, but every time I go to stand up some bugger grabs me by the "Niagaras".'

Fearing his little mate was in real trouble, Lillee kicked the door open.

One look at the scene inside and Dennis doubled up in laughter. 'You silly bugger, you're sitting on the mop bucket!'

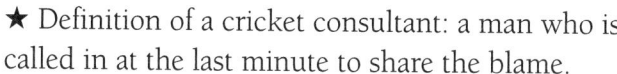

★ Definition of a cricket consultant: a man who is called in at the last minute to share the blame.

★ Two wicket keepers died and went to heaven. St Peter said, 'Anyone who has ever cheated or appealed without reason or sledged a batsman step forward and ask for forgiveness.'

One stepped forward and asked for forgiveness. St Peter said, 'Come on in, and bring that other deaf bastard with you.'

★ How do you recognise an Australian cricketer at Lord's?

He's the one holding the ashes.

★ Australia played Jamaica at the Sabina Park Cricket Ground before the first Test match of the 1973 tour. As usual it had been a very long, hot day and I was approaching my twenty-fifth eight ball over—I needed a drink!

My prayers were answered under a cloudless sky that afternoon. The perspiration was leaking from my body like a dripping tap—not one part of my cricket attire was dry.

One guy screamed, 'Wokko, ya wanna drink of my rum?' I tried to explain to him that if the fellow at first slip with the baggy green cap on his head, Ian Chappell, saw me drinking his rum, I would never play cricket for Australia again.

His reply was, 'Ee won't see ya man!' And with that remark, the big black man turned to his mate in the back row of the bamboo grandstand. He let out a piercing whistle to catch his friend's attention. Immediately a huge black umbrella was relayed overhead to my new pal in the front row. His name was George.

Before I knew it the umbrella had been thrust through the fence and opened to a diameter of about six foot. I thought to myself, 'There is no way known anyone will be able to spot me having a drink now.'

Through the fence came a dirty, grotty, green bottle of home-made rum. I looked carefully at the neck of the bottle—it was not too flash! Keith Miller well may have been the last Aussie to drink from it.

Then all the possibilities ran across my mind. I could just have a little sip straight from the bottle—not exactly safe. Maybe if I just dipped my finger in the top of the rum bottle it would be OK. Finally I said, 'Bugger it, I'll go for the whole catastrophe!' And I did. With the black umbrella for protection, I squatted down on my haunches, and drank.

The home-made brew must have been about 500 per cent proof—bloody unreal! I could feel the warm liquid sting on its rapid journey to my stomach. It was a strange burning, searing sensation. My Aussie cap almost jumped off the top of my head—this was good stuff, 'oh yeah, oh yeah!'

The majority of the mob behind me stood up and cheered. Some of their very colourful hats and caps were thrown high in the air above their heads. (How they got them back, I really don't know.)

With all this noise, people spun round to see what was happening. I had already handed back the brew to George, who was attempting to dismantle his mate's very large black brolly, but not without a lot of trouble. From where I stood, it was very difficult to tell the difference between some bent umbrella spokes and the barbed wire fence itself.

I slowly walked away from the crowd as though nothing had happened. The skipper saw nothing odd and had nothing to say.

Two overs later, when I was fielding again in front of my friends in the primitive bamboo stand, things began to happen.

A batsman named Maurice Foster had hit a lofted hook shot behind square leg. The ball hung in the air for a long time. With all the pace I didn't possess, I managed to get close enough to attempt a diving right-handed catch. Without exaggerating, I must have run 40 metres around the boundary line to pull off the catch—it was magnificent. I even rolled over an extra couple of times, after coming to ground heavily, so as to make the effort look even more spectacular.

The masses erupted as I came to my feet. Every second bloke in the stand swayed to his right as if to mimic the catch. I felt obliged to acknowledge the crowd. Obviously it was not my natural pace and ability that enabled me to take the ball safely—it had to be the home-made rum I'd been given! So I began furiously rubbing my hand around in a circular movement over my stomach to show the effects of the jungle juice. Again the crowd roared in acceptance.

At this stage I had my back to the centre wicket area and began really playing to the rowdy, colourful spectators. I was enjoying myself when a deathly SILENCE settled across the entire ground. I must have been the only person at the ground who didn't realise that it had been called a NO BALL, and the batsmen had just completed three runs.

★ It is rumoured that a Test cricketer once remarked, 'When you bat with Graeme Wood you don't call—you pray!'

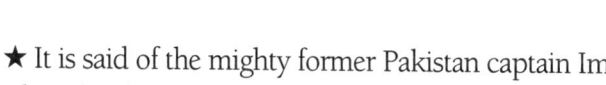

★ It is said of the mighty former Pakistan captain Imran Khan that he is the only player to call his partner for a run and wish him good luck at the same time.

★ What did out-of-form Australian captain Mark Taylor say when he was run out in the lead-up match prior to the 1997 Ashes Test series?

'Shall I leave out the swear words?'

'Yes.'

He never spoke, but courageously scored perhaps the most important century of his career in the First Test . . . a week later!

★ The young batsman was apologising to his captain for scoring yet another duck.

'Perhaps I should have another net.'

'Well, make it a fishing one!'

★ A player can't stroll out of the Sydney Cricket Ground at 10.30 p.m. and expect to be asleep by 11.15 p.m., all neatly tucked away in the hotel cot. Everyone needs to 'unwind' a little.

Australians, being the committed sportsmen they always have been, will hurry back to the hotel where the team stays and most probably relax over a cappuccino and hamburger.

On the other hand the 'Calypso Kids' will be more interested in a party . . . any party! And in every city on the touring calendar involving a West Indian team, there will inevitably be 'the party'.

For example, after a day/night clash at the SCG, the typical invitation to 'party' predictably arrived in the form of a folded piece of paper via the twelfth man. He's the guy who had spent the entire evening scrutinising the state of play outside the fence— up periscope. The ball bearings in the neck of Bernard Julien were working overtime scanning the grandstands for potential party goers of the female kind.

The unanimous team decision after a comfortable limited over win was: 'YES, we'll be in it!'

The venue was North Sydney, over the Harbour Bridge and turn left. Inside it was standing room only . . . wall to wall women and a hyperactive, winning team—the chemistry was ideal, the music very up tempo and a truckload of rum 'n' cola to quench the thirst.

The Master Blaster, Viv Richards, was playing the old bull . . . he didn't have a sign above the gate, but he might as well have, saying: I am available.

Desmond Haynes, one of the happiest cricketers ever to pull on a pad, had more moves than Warwick Capper when he spearheaded the Sydney Swans forward line many, many seasons back. And you couldn't forget the human clothes peg—Joel Garner. The big fella had a wonderful vantage point, head and shoulders above the crush . . . and an easy swig of his drink.

The hours danced by and the level in the various varieties of bottles drained steadily . . . but all good parties come to an end. It was 3.00 a.m.

The captain of the side, Clive Lloyd, a charismatic gentleman, used his authority to maintain discipline: 'Right boys, that's it, back to the pub!'

The first vehicle to depart contained Viv and Joel. Obviously the 'big bird' wasn't driving—his 200 cm frame wouldn't fold under the steering wheel—Viv was in control.

Joel had left in a hurry and was feeling the pressure. The giant fast bowler was desperate for a 'you 'n' me'—legs crossed, arms crossed and maybe even his fingers. But all the crossing in the world wasn't going to relieve the agony of a bursting bladder.

Just before the halfway mark of the bridge the passenger shouted: 'Stop the car man . . . stop the car!' So out they stepped. It was so dark, nobody could see them. Like two large silhouettes, they stood at the balcony of Australia's famous landmark, admiring the reflections of the moonlight on the water below. First to address the problem was Joel: 'Gee, the water's cold tonight Viv!' he confessed.

With the recoil of an elephant gun, the world's finest wielder of a willow replied: 'And it's not that deep either, is it Bird?'

★ 'You may not like me now', said the new player, 'but I grow on people.'

And a voice from the back, 'Of course you do, you little wart.'

★ He was a Melbourne-based cricketer but loved playing Shield matches in Perth because he had relations there.

Unfortunately his wife found out who with!

★ Greg Matthews was different, as we all know, But how different?

Well, he was the only cricketer to tour India and suffer from constipation.

★ On their one night off the touring Australian cricket team went to a Muslim nightclub, and watched them dance sheik to sheik.

★ He said, 'I'm sorry I'm late for training coach but my dad got burned.'

'Oh I'm sorry. Is it serious?'

'Oh well, they don't mess around at the crematorium.'

★ He said to the committee, 'Next Saturday, I'd like to open the batting. I'd like to open the bowling, and I'd like to captain the side.'

It was just another case of putting all his 'begs' in one 'askit'.

★ My old man was captain of a social team selected from patrons of the Empire Hotel—he was the proprietor and of course supplied the liquid refreshments.

As you may well imagine the best cricket in these games is played late in the day when all the Dutch courage and confidence emerges. But not always with success.

The Sunday's proceedings went along very well, especially the morning session. Everyone had fun and a drink or two.

When someone finally tallied up the score card (on the back of a piece of cardboard) we became aware of an intriguing situation. The Empire Hotel needed 10 runs to win, and importantly, there were two balls remaining. Possible but improbable!

I could sense the atmosphere around the ground. Everyone momentarily put down their amber-filled glasses in anticipation. Kids stopped playing and the dogs began howling.

The opposition bowler charged in to bowl off an unusually long run, his pocket full of car keys sounding like an eccentric belting away on a xylophone. I can still see the frenzied look on his purple-red face after running so far just to deliver one ball—a sort of distorted agony and ecstasy!

Big Max was 'on strike' and I was at the bowler's end, backing up on nought, not out! The senior partner immediately moved onto the front foot . . . his size-twelve sandshoes not quite to the pitch of the ball, but nevertheless his eyes were focused clearly on the well-worn cherry. It was so worn out that it looked more like a rag doll than a cricket ball.

The attempted cover drive wasn't exactly a reproduction from Sir Donald Bradman's *Art of Cricket*. My father's flashing blade could only manage a thick inside edge and the ball gently rolled away behind the square leg umpire, towards the fence. We both took off and ran like hell, turned for 2, looked for 3, even 4. When it came to the sixth run, I said to my partner, 'That's it, dad, we can only run 6!'

'Don't stop now, son,' he replied, 'just keep on running!' And so we did!

While we were scampering for runs . . . four or five fieldsmen had gathered in the long grass down by the fine leg boundary. Dad and I just kept our heads down and continued running. By the time we'd run all 10 necessary to win the game, about eight guys were stooped in a circle about 60 metres off the bat, at long leg.

My dad was suffering from a distinct lack of fitness—it's not every day a batsman gets to run 10 in a row. We'd won the match with a ball to spare!

Before we left the pitch, curiosity got the better of us . . . there were now ten players standing in a tight circle at deep fine leg, up to their ankles in grass.

And there it was—the lonely old cricket ball dead smack in the middle of a curled-up tiger snake. There was absolutely no way known that any of those blokes was going to put his hand down to pick up the ball! Not a hero among them!

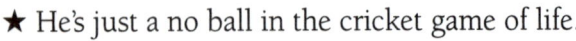

★ He's just a no ball in the cricket game of life.

★ He was in and out of the national side for years, so it is no wonder that when asked who was the greatest opponent he had faced he said, 'The Australian selectors.'

★ Allan Border once hit six sixes off an Irish bowler in Dublin. In the same game the bowler was out for a duck. If the Irish player had been a Pom he would have been regarded as an all-rounder.

★ End-of-season trip. The hotel manager is complaining about player behaviour.

The major culprit is defending himself, 'I resent the implication that I was drunk and set the bed on fire. That bed was on fire when I got into it.'

★ In the mid-1980s the Australian cricket team was beaten by New Zealand and going through a bad time. At the after-game dinner after one particularly heavy defeat the chairman said, 'Ladies and gentlemen, in conclusion I would like to raise your glasses and drink to absent friends and in that I include the names of the complete Australian batting line-up.'

★ At the age of about eleven or twelve I was lucky enough to play cricket in the same team as my old man. I should tell you that curators in Tasmania are not too flash. They turn up about every three months to cut the grass. And even though this particular game was a Grand Final—Mathinna versus Oatlands—I don't think anyone would have seen the match . . . it certainly wasn't televised.

And just because it was a Grand Final made no difference to the fact that there had been two and a half months between hair cuts—the grass stood about a metre high.

The situation didn't worry me because I had the ability to hit the ball in the air, but some of our other players were a little bit inhibited by this sea of green.

So, imagine the scene at the ground. Thirty-five of our relations and their dogs have turned up. The buzz; the barking; the horns tooting all the way around the ground . . . you can feel the tension.

We required 17 runs to win. Normally we would romp in. But this time, it's just a little bit tight. There's only ONE ball remaining.

And to make matters worse, there's only one batsman left: my old man. Just how good a player is Big Max, to be batting number 11 behind me in a Sunday afternoon competition?

The state of play doesn't improve. The previous batsman to be dismissed has chopped down so hard on a yorker, he's broken the handle of the only bat in the club.

We used to drop the bat and run up and down in between wickets in those days. There was no Kerry Packer back then, and sponsorship was unheard of.

No way was the opposition going to lend us their

only bat. The old man walked out the gate, grabbed a picket from the fence, confidently strolled to the wicket and took block. My old man is a dead-set impostor. He possesses one shot and one shot only, and that is a slog straight down the ground.

Fair dinkum, my old man would not be good enough to snick a ball to Third Man. Still, the opposition were not going to let him off lightly—no matter what the odds!

The fast bowler's got the ball in his hand and is giving it heaps. He's polishing her up and down; really is giving it plenty!

Now I should mention there's a lot of science involved in polishing a cricket ball: Total maximum utilisation of one half of a cricket ball up and down your trousers, right?

I've been involved with my body for a fair while now and I can't come up with a better groove than that for polishing a cricket ball. Agree? The action's not just for women watching colour telly. It's for real!

Every fast bowler worth his salt has been known to rub a cricket ball up and down his trousers. Apart from one, Jeffrey Thomson. Thommo holds the ball in front, belt buckle high and gives it the gyrating pelvic girdle.

In the fast bowler charges, through the long grass. Up high on the toe-nails in the delivery stride (Tasmanians have got real long toe nails). With a huge grunt he lets the ball go and the old man gives him the big Colgate smile back down the track.

I'm not out at the other end playing for the 'red inks' (not out). Now anyone who knows anything at all about the game of cricket will realise . . . you must NOT bowl a ball pitched middle or leg stump to a tail-end batsman, OK? Otherwise you'll end up being hit straight down the ground on the first bounce for 4, or depending on how much right hand is on the bat . . . a whack through mid-wicket for 6!

So what does this bloke do? He bowls the big rank, half volley—didn't swing a lot because there's not much red paint left on the ball. And like most number 11 batsmen, the old man plays straight down the track. Plonk. Almost trod on the ball, which has got to be a bonus. Where do you think the ball's landed? Pitched middle and leg stump!!

So the old man's hit through the most magnificent on drive you've ever seen. We take off, run 1, 2, 3, 4, 5 . . . and there are five guys out at long-on. Can't find the ball anywhere in the long grass.

As we crossed for 6 I said to my partner: 'Dad, that's it. You can only run 6.' He said: 'Bullshit son, keep running, keep running.'

7, 8, 9, 10 and there are now eight fieldsmen way out at long-on and can't find the ball anywhere.

11, 12, 13. The old man has now got heartburn, dyspepsia, the whole catastrophe. You just don't come in first ball in a Grand Final and chip 13 off your toes, do you? I mean, that is really not on . . . no matter what grade of cricket.

14, 15, 16 . . . There are now ten of 'em out there at long-on . . . and still can't find the ball anywhere.

The wicketkeeper is the only bloke left— standing over the stumps for the run out. The rest of them are stamping down the long grass with their boots. A quarter of the ground is trodden absolutely flat. The rest of the grass is a metre high.

17 runs. What a fantastic performance! To get up and win the Grand Final, another flag for the dressing-sheds back home . . . against the odds. You beauty!

Great sportsman that he was, the old man, looked across to the opposition captain, who was a bloody long way away at long-on, walked in his direction.

'Do you really want to know where the ball is?' he asked with a grin.

Then he turned over the picket . . . and wedged deep into a nail at the end of the piece of timber was the lost cricket ball . . . Could only happen in Tasmania!

★ A coach has to be a diplomat, particularly when he has to drop a former great player.

'Well, Dean,' he said, 'I don't know how on earth we'll manage without you, but as from next week we're going to have to try.'

★ The captain had just told the team his game plan and he concluded with the following. 'All right lads, that's the game plan. You may think it's a case of six of one and half a dozen of the other, but I assure you it is nothing of the sort. In fact it is exactly the opposite.'

★ In America winning at baseball is an obsession. In Britain winning at cricket is an odd occurrence.

★ A lucky batsman is one who is scoring more runs than you are.

★ Cricket coaches are all right in their place. (From the M4 Motorway)

★ He's a great bowler, really great. So accurate that he hits the bat every time.

★ He had a few too many drinks at lunch. He then went in to bat and he could see three balls. So he decided that he would hit the middle one.

Unfortunately he was clean bowled because he had used his outside bat.

★ I once bowled against Bradman and I had him in two minds. He didn't know whether to hit me for four or for six.

★ He walks into his doctor's office. He sits down and says, 'Listen Doc, I have a problem. I can't bat, I can't bowl, I can't field. What can I do?'

The doctor said, 'You're a bit overanxious, in fact you are very much over-reacting. Just have a few days off.'

He replied, 'I can't. I'm playing Test cricket for England at Lord's tomorrow.'

★ My problem is that when I'm batting I always seem to be in the middle of a hat-trick.

★ At the club's annual talent quest all the batsmen got together as a band.

The opening batsman said, 'Well, don't bother with me—I wouldn't know a trumpet from a trombone.'

The captain said, 'That's all right. We don't have a string section.'

★ I am totally loyal to my captain. I support him when he is right.

I keep quiet the other 95 per cent of the time.

★ The new Australian fast bowler was summoned before the A.C.B. It is said that he kicked an umpire, knocked two batsmen unconscious and stuffed the stumps down a third batsman's throat.

Former fast bowler Dennis Lillee has branded him a sissy.

★ They think so much of Dennis Lillee in New Zealand that they have just named a mountain after him. It's called 'Why Kick a Paki'.

★ The best way to get the Poms to beat the West Indies is to get them to change their name to Australia.

★ 'Tell me, do any of your fellow selectors suffer from insanity?'

'No,' he said. 'They all seem to enjoy it.'

★ A batsman once said that Jeff Thomson's second delivery is the nicest to watch, because it means that he has survived his first one.

★ They once asked the chairman of the Australian selectors if he had ever been wrong. He thought about it for a minute and then responded, 'Yes, once, years ago. I thought that I had made a wrong decision. Of course it turned out to have been the right decision all along. But I was wrong to have thought that I could have been wrong.'

★ He said he was not a conceited player but the local council did offer him two million dollars if they could pull down his ego and build a shopping centre.

★ He had a great capacity for taking wickets and an even greater capacity for taking praise.

★ They said he was the worst captain that the club had ever had. That was a lie because he wasn't that good.

★ It was a cricket match between the monsters and the vampires.

The vampires won the toss and Dracula went in as first bat.

★ He has an enormous capacity for beer.

Unfortunately he keeps getting drunk before he reaches it.

★ He arrived late for cricket practice and the coach was furious.

'Why are you late?' he asked.

'Well,' he answered, 'I was late when I started from home.'

'Well, why didn't you start earlier?'

'Because it was too late to start earlier.'

★ Having five cricket selectors is a touching belief in the collective wisdom of individual ignorance.

★ He saw a female streaker at the MCG. So to be different, he ran fully clothed through a nudist camp.

★ Forget Russian Roulette, the game is Cricket Roulette: six chambers, six bullets and you put the gun to a cricket selector's head.

★ He was by far the oldest player on the cricket team, and despite family pleadings he wouldn't retire.

In fact he said the only day he wouldn't play was August 23rd because that was the day he went for his annual autopsy.

★ No wonder he was always late for training—he was born on his mother's way home from the hospital.

★ Greg Chappell would agree that for him, playing matches against New Zealand hasn't been without its problems—for example the notorious underarm incident at the MCG.

Then, after the First Test debacle of 1985—a loss by an innings and 41 runs in Brisbane—the Kiwis caused him a few more sleepless nights, this time as a national selector. I've still got very vivid memories of an incident during the second Test match against New Zealand at Auckland way back in 1977.

Greg invited NZ to bat first on a rain-affected wicket at Eden Park. Australia exploited the difficult conditions to limit the Kiwis to a first innings total of 229.

I'm sure our captain was looking for a score of 350 plus and a lead of 150 on the first innings . . .

and proceedings were going nicely for our boys until just before tea on the second day.

It was an overcast day and a maximum temperature of about 5 degrees Celsius was forecast. Then it all started happening . . . a heavy dark cloud of smoke wafted across the ground from a house at the rear of the grandstand. The fire must have been serious because I remember the piercing shrill of a fire-engine ringing in my ears. As a batsman you really don't need that sort of interference to your concentration at the precise moment a bowler like Richard Hadlee lets the ball go.

Using the smokescreen for distraction a streaker pranced out on to the Rugby Union ground-cum-Test match venue, from the seated area in the northern section.

After jumping the fence and conducting a brief 'fashion' parade, he returned to his cheering audience. As he hurdled the white picket fence, arms raised in triumph, I thought he might do himself a nasty injury. No such luck. He regained his seat—still starkers.

With only minutes remaining before tea, NZ captain Glen Turner decided to give spinner Hedley Howarth a bowl. And while the bowler was busy stepping out his run up, another well-sozzled streaker bounded across the ground from the northern end of Eden Park.

This chap was 'well-dressed' though. He wore an impressive suntan, goose-pimpled bum, a pair of heavy leather boots, socks and a pale blue towelling hat. As he raced past the square leg umpire he flung his hat into the air in victory then disappeared over the wire gate at the southern end and into the carpark. . . hotly pursued by a policeman.

I could see both Greg and Rick McCosker getting more and more agitated by these unexpected happenings. After just a couple of deliveries . . . streaker number 1 was back over the fence again. Full of confidence and 'ink'.

So excited by the performance of master batsman Greg Chappell was he, the naked nutter wanted to shake the great man by the hand.

Incidentally, he was sporting a pair of radio

headphones so he could hear a ball by ball description of his antics.

He had soared over the fence, evading Richard Hadlee at square leg, and continued lumbering towards our captain . . . who by this time was furious and staring glassy eyed at the naked man. The strokeplayers' famous double scoop Gray Nicholls bat was raised above his head . . .

You see, Greg Chappell has never quite felt the same about streakers after an incident in a Shield match the previous year. Three women promptly paraded naked towards Greg and his not out partner . . . on the centre wicket area at the WACA ground in Perth.

From what Greg told me, one of them had beautiful eyes. Though his mate tells me he wasn't looking at their eyes when he asked them to 'hang around and have a chat'.

Incredibly it all backfired when the 'young lady' that Greg fancied turned out to be a female impersonator. The man was shattered!

The whole exercise had been a publicity stunt for

a local night club—similar to the brazen young blonde who bared it all in front of 100,000 people at a VFL grand final at the MCG a few years later.

Since being so 'wrong' it would be fair to say that streakers have never been his favourite people.

But back to New Zealand . . . in Greg's mind this bloke was jeopardising Australia's aim of batting through the session without losing a wicket.

So Greg grabbed the man by his out-stretched hand and gave him a solid spanking across his polar bear white bottom . . . WHACK, WHACK, WHACK! Colour quickly returned to his bum.

Greg informed the intruder he was definitely not impressed. The streaker mentioned something about poking the cord from his earphones in Greg's ear-holes. This brought yet another couple of belts from the master's flashing blade!

By this time the policemen were in position and the offender was apprehended as he charged off in the direction of the seat he left vacant.

Next delivery, McCosker hit the ball firmly to mid-on but Chappell, thinking there wasn't a run in it, turned his back. Rick kept on running and was unfortunately run out at the striker's end by wicket-keeper Jock Edwards.

A disappointed Chappell left the field with his head hung low. The streaker was escorted out of the ground. Australia had now lost its second wicket.

At stumps that night, Inspector George Dwan, one of the policemen who arrested the streaker, searched out Greg for a chat.

When the inspector entered the dressing room, everyone shut up, silence reigned supreme. He said: 'Son, you ought to be ashamed of what happened out there!'

Greg replied: 'Hang on a minute, you mean the streaker don't you?'

The policeman answered: 'No, absolutely disgusting,' with a certain sense of finality about the comment.

Greg looked blankly at the inspector and said, 'Why?'

The answer is the moral to this story: 'Here you are, you play four cross bat shots,' illustrating with a movement of his arms as if to play a pull-shot, 'when one straight drive would have done the trick!' And he followed through as if to play a big straight drive at an imaginary streaker!

★ Greg Chappell, who had a string of ducks in an illustrious international career, once told me that he started to call his bat Polo, because it had a hole in the middle.

★ Life is so unfair, particularly at a cricket wedding. If the groom is a batsman his team-mates will use their bats to form an arch as he leaves the church.

But what can they use if he's a bowler?

★ The game was so bad and boring that even the empty seats asked for their money back.

★ Let's face it, Kerry Packer is not your average working-class cricket supporter. In fact when he has a tea break at the game Allan Border comes over to pour it.

★ The old school boy, Classic: 'Doctor, I feel like a cricket bat.'

The Doctor: 'How's that?'

★ It was one of those games that was so bad, it was taped in front of a dead audience.

★ 'Wasn't my fault,' said the bowler. 'I had seven catches dropped today.'

And the captain said, 'You're not wrong . . . all by people in the stand.'

★ The ground announcer at a game of County cricket: 'For the benefit of the players, here are the names of the spectators.'

★ My last word on Lillee and Thommo goes to the English Test batsman, who asked the umpire to move the sight-screen.

'Where to?' asked the umpire

The batsman said, 'Between me and those two mad bastards—Lillee and Thomson.'

★ Rodney Marsh, on his first visit to London, said to the MCC type (handlebar moustache, egg yolk and ketchup tie, pinstripe suit), 'Um where's the dressing room at?'

And the MCC type said, 'You colonials, don't you know you can't end a sentence with a preposition?'

And former school teacher Marsh said, 'You're quite right. Where's the dressing room at, wanker?'

★ Team-mate of Merv Hughes: 'Merv's so excited at being a father because there are now twice as many new toys in the house to play with!'

★ Ground announcer: 'And now, Merv Hughes runs up to the crease and about to bowl with a new ball.'

Marvellous what doctors can do these days.

★ Ashes to ashes
  Dust to dust,
  If Lillee doesn't get you,
  Then Thommo must!

★ The last English-speaking cab driver in Sydney obviously wasn't a cricket enthusiast. It was like seeing the lights on in a house yet knowing there was no one home!

He still hadn't recognised either of us and right in the middle of a mega cricket controversy! Maybe this guy didn't look at billboards, television or the front page of a newspaper. Maybe he couldn't read. Then again Marshie's head is unmistakable—a one off.

'What do ya do for a living?' he rambled on automatically, not really interested in the answer.

'We're both professional cricketers!' Rodney grizzled. The enlightened cabbie nodded casually.

Now I could tell from the next deep and meaningful question that he knew his cricket really well: 'Who do you play for?'

How many professional cricket teams are there in Australia?

'I play for Australia and WA,' Rod growled through his bristling moustache, 'and the big gorilla in the back seat . . . he plays for Victoria and Australia.'

'Aw! Right!' Finally after drip-feeding this fascinating sports fanatic the penny dropped. 'You blokes . . . you were in that underarm game, weren't ya, yesterday at the MCG?'

He was a different person with a couple of right answers. He went through about four sets of red lights over the next few minutes, as he kept exercising the ball bearings in his neck looking at his passenger. And every time Rod's moustache bristled a bit more. I knew they didn't like one another a lot.

He looked at Marshie once more in the morning light. 'So what do you do mate, bat or bowl?'

★ Alan McGilvray once gave me some invaluable advice.

'Son,' he said, 'if you imagine you are talking to a blind man when describing the game you will do allright—call it colour radio.'

Because of their talents it would appear to listeners that there are rarely problems . . . but let me share a few occasions where things didn't quite work out as planned!

In fact the Australia v West Indies limited over match mentioned earlier was just the beginning of several testing moments.

The ABC radio commentator's box in those days was not the most aesthetically pleasing piece of architecture at the Melbourne Cricket Ground. Located at the back of the cigar smokers stand (MCC members) it resembled a crude chook house on the top level—split level over two seats approximately two metres by three metres—with a corrugated iron roof but without the wire mesh (sliding glass windows) front.

On that unforgettable day the temperature

hovered around 45 degrees Celsius—very, very hot!

In order to occupy my position at the microphone as expert comments man, I had to climb bodily over the shoulders of both Mac and our ever-reliable master of statistics, Jack Cameron. With a nick-name like Tanglefoot, standing 6'4" tall and sending the rev counter on the scales racing towards seventeen stone I was never going to achieve my objective without incident. Even the doorway into the confined space presented a struggle—it sloped across the top from right to left about 5' to 3'6".

I felt like a dog entering his kennel. My leading knee cap clipped dear old Mac smack bang on the back of his head . . . the pair of binoculars he was holding went close to shattering his reading glasses and the veteran student of the game almost swallowed the cigarette he was enjoying. I knew I was in trouble when he started coughing with an unhealthy barking sound. Step number two got me into more strife. Remember there were no Unisys computers spitting out green figures on a backlit screen in those days— Jack either stored them in his head or in several shoe boxes that he never let out of his sight (fifty years of accumulated averages, aggregates and match results painstakingly handwritten onto small cards). As my size eleven shoe landed on the lid of his priceless shoe box, our scorer let out an almighty shout in disbelief. While his words echoed around the Members Stand . . . cards spewed out onto the rows of spectators like a pack of cards. Two out of two . . . and the new boy still had a pace to go.

No commercial breaks on the ABC . . . the broadcast box was in a state of upheaval. Mac and Jack eyeballed the intruder with looks that could send a keen mind blank. The two technicians were trying desperately to suppress uncontrollable bouts of laughter.

By the time I finally sank into my seat my nerves were shot . . . but both forgave me in a big hurry and 'nursed' me through the next hour together. Somehow it was difficult not to think about who called the first hour—batting legend Norm O'Neill. Now Norm is the sort of bloke who enjoys a drink *even* on a cold day . . . The pair of headphones had filled like cups with stale sweat 'n' beer . . . as I exercised my jaw Norm's stay in the box trickled down my neck and lingered longer than any aftershave.

My new Pierre Cardin suit, especially purchased for the occasion, looked as if I had been swimming in it! Bad luck about the under armpit odour—even Aerogard wouldn't have worked in these conditions!

★ Sir Donald Bradman is walking through the Adelaide Hills when a ferocious storm suddenly erupts. Sir Don slips and breaks his leg, but he's saved by his trusty German Shepherd that half drags and half carries him to the nearest farm house.

Sir Donald hammers on the door asking to be admitted. The lady of the house refuses point blank to admit either Sir Donald or the dog, until Sir Don pleads, 'Madam, think of the consequences you wouldn't turn a knight out on dog like this.'

★ At the country game in Wagga the batsman disputed being given out, and the umpire gave him that well known retort, 'If you don't believe me, look in the local Wagga paper tomorrow and you'll see you were out.'

'You look,' shouted the batsman, 'because I'm the editor.'

★ When Ian Healy got his three-hundredth Test wicket a lady said to him, 'I was so excited I nearly fell out of the stand.'

And Ian said, 'The way I played today, I would have caught you as well.'

★ Sir Don is strolling across the hallowed turf of Adelaide Oval in his famous interview with Ray Martin.

Ray asked, 'Sir Donald, how do you think you would fare against today's English bowlers?'

And Sir Donald replies, 'I would probably average between 50 and 60.'

Ray says, 'But Sir Donald, your Test average is 99.99.'

And the great man replies mischievously, 'But Ray, you must remember I am 86 years of age,' as he stroked his chin and began to smirk.

★ The smallest cricket team in the world: Mountbatten, Stan Bowls and W.C. Fields.

★ He was not the most intelligent of cricket managers as he told the bowlers to pair off in threes.

★ We laugh at our wives who cry over problems of actors in soap operas. I've no doubt it must be of great wonder to them how we can get so excited when a person we have never met hits a six.

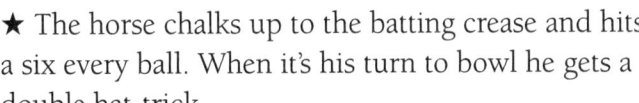

★ The horse chalks up to the batting crease and hits a six every ball. When it's his turn to bowl he gets a double hat-trick.

The team manager is over the moon. 'You can bat and bowl. Can you field?'

The horse said, 'If I could run I wouldn't be here, I'd be in the Melbourne Cup.'

★ In one game he dropped eight catches. The captain was understandably annoyed.

'Today,' he said, 'you fielded like a pregnant

woman trying to pole vault. And as for dropping eight catches—if you were a fish, you would be allergic to water.'

★ 'Well, let me tell you how they played: they dropped every ball, they fielded like penguins, their bowlers couldn't bowl and the batsmen couldn't bat.

'If they'd have played any worse they would have had to ask the Governor for a pardon.'

★ After the first trial match of the season the chairman of selectors said to the young man, 'Young man, the sporting skills you showed today indicate that your best opportunities in cricket lie with a club—where your father holds an influential position.'

★ It there is anything to reincarnation, she wants to come back as a cricket ball.

She'd do anything to be rubbed by Shane Warne.

★ Bob Hawke, Labor's longest serving Prime Minister and sports lover extraordinaire, was batting for the Prime Minister's XI.

The wicket keeper began to sledge him unmercifully, so much so that Mr Hawke was approached by the umpire, who asked, 'Mr Prime Minister do you want me to report him?'

And Hawkey thought for a moment and said, 'I'm in somewhat of a dilemma. If what he is saying is from one cricketer to another, then of course he should be reported. If, however, what he is saying, he is saying to the Prime Minister of Australia, then that is his constitutional right.'

★ Perhaps it was the same player of whom somebody once said, 'Giving him a cricket bat is like giving a Stradivarius to King Kong.'

★ Greg Matthews and Graham Gooch by their television commercials have really made people aware of transplants. So they got a bit of a surprise when they said to the bald Rugby union player, 'Why don't you get a transplant?'

The player said, 'That's bloody ridiculous. How stupid would I look going around with a kidney on the top of my head?'

★ He is one of the true legends of modern cricket—equally at home batting or bowling, or endorsing products.

★ Went on three Ashes tours, and he was so neat, and so tidy, he never left the hotel without having his bed maid.

★ The Australian cricketer on the Ashes tour who had a reputation for having a preference for ladies from the aristocracy was asked by a reporter, 'Is it true that you have been misbehaving?'

And the cricketer replied, 'In what manor sir?'

★ Dennis Lillee and Rodney Marsh had one of the greatest bowler–wicket keeper combinations of all time.

Their system was very simple. If Dennis raised one finger, it meant it was his fast ball. If he raised two fingers, it was a slightly slower ball. And if he raised three fingers it meant 'Rodney, the cameras are on you, for God's sake, stop scratching yourself.'

★ He received his first Test cap, and in the dressing room he said to the more experienced player: 'Hey, this cap is too big for me.'

And the player said, 'Just make sure it stays that way, too!'

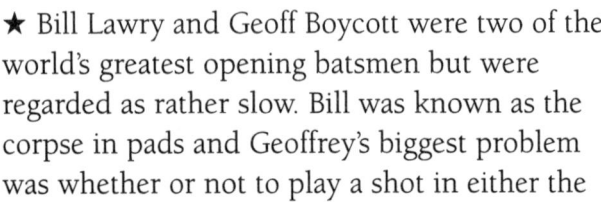

★ The selector says, 'You were bowling like lightning today.'

Fast bowler says, 'You mean I'm fast?'

'No, you never strike in the same place twice.'

★ Bill Lawry and Geoff Boycott were two of the world's greatest opening batsmen but were regarded as rather slow. Bill was known as the corpse in pads and Geoffrey's biggest problem was whether or not to play a shot in either the first or second hour of a Test match.

In fact it was said that if by some accident of birth they had opened the batting together, they could have made the one day game last a month.

★ Bill Lawry, in spite of his rather dour image as a batsman, is one of the funniest after-dinner speakers I've ever heard. He's not afraid to send himself up.

In particular, he refers to his rather prominent nose, saying that he first realised it was big when leaving a premiere of the *Elephant Man*. People kept asking him for his autograph.

★ Two signs at the MCG. One is on a single bedsheet draped over the edge of the concrete stand: 'Bill Lawry's handkerchief'.

The other: 'Bill, if your brains were in your nose you'd be a genius.'

★ It was the worst wicket keeping display of all time: six dropped catches, fifty extras, regularly collided with the slip fielders. He apologised to the team.

'I think I need some help. What coach would you recommend?'

As one voice, they replied, 'A long-distance one.'

★ The little boy had been so obviously ill treated— black and blue, suffering from malnutrition.

The welfare authorities took his parents to court. The parents were jailed and the judge granted custody of the boy to the English cricket team because as he said, 'They haven't beaten anyone in years.'

★ To the treasurer of one county club struggling financially, 'Do you try to live within your income?'

He replied, 'We can't even live within our credit.'

★ After a pretty bad Test match coach Bob Simpson addresses the Australian cricket team.

'Gentlemen, swinging the bat is great enjoyment. It is beautiful to watch, it is fine exercise, it strengthens the shoulders and besides that, one day, one of you may hit the ball.'

★ Did you ever get the feeling that some journalists' reports of a game have the same ring of truth as a sex manual written by a eunuch?

★ There was once the King Edward potato that fell in love with Alan McGilvray, and told his parents that he wanted to marry him. His parents said, 'Don't be ridiculous, you're a king, Edward. He is only a common-tator.'

★ 'My sister thinks you are the greatest cricketer in all the world.'

'Oh, thank you very much I'd love to meet her.'

'I'm sorry, you can't do that. We never let her out of her room.'

★ The hypnotist calls for a volunteer from the audience. The man comes on the stage, the hypnotist puts him in a trance and tells him he's to act like a dog, which he does—running around the stage on all fours and barking.

The hypnotist snaps his fingers and the man comes back to his senses.

He then puts the second volunteer into a trace and tells her to conduct the orchestra for three minutes. She conducts the imaginary orchestra with all the energy of a professional conductor.

The hypnotist snaps his fingers and the lady comes back to her senses.

The third volunteer steps up on the stage and is immediately put into a trance. The hypnotist says, 'You are now bowling for Australia against the Poms in the Boxing Day Test. In your first over you have taken five wickets for no runs. The Poms are nine wickets down for no runs. 100,000 people are screaming . . . waiting for you to come on to bowl your ball.'

And at that point the man slowly opens one eye, stares at the hypnotist and says, 'You snap your fingers now mate, and I'll break every bone in your body.'

★ 'Greg Matthews really is different.'
'How different?'
'Well, if he was a masochist he'd take painkillers.'

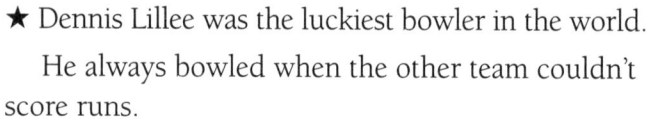

★ Dennis Lillee was the luckiest bowler in the world.
He always bowled when the other team couldn't score runs.

★ A series of events during the 1973 Australian tour of the West Indies had us in stitches of laughter . . . even if they did cause some of the locals a slight embarrassment. This story really should be known as the 'tale of the President's dog', and not surprisingly centres around that irrepressible character D. K. Lillee.

Lillee had developed a stunt which involved

scaring the daylights out of the drivers who ferried us around in the team bus. The buses we used had wooden slatted seats and no windows. In fact, very tinny conveyances all round.

One day our driver had been manoeuvring to squeeze the bus through a pair of large gate pillars, with plenty of encouragement from the lads.

Dennis leaned out of the window and nearly belted a hole in the red metal panelling with his fist. The sound was like a bomb exploding, and someone yelled 'You've hit the bloody post you stupid fool!'

The poor driver slammed on the brakes, stalled the bus and was quickly out of the seat and around to inspect the damage, looking as if he was to face an execution squad for his folly. Of course he couldn't understand why there was still a good six inches of clearance between the bus and the post when he had clearly heard a crash.

Eventually he began to get the message, and even saw the funny side.

On another occasion when we were on a

shopping expedition, Lillee and the same bus driver cooked up a bit of a stunt between them.

A very old jalopy was parked in the spot where the bus driver was supposed to be, so Lillee persuaded the driver to drive as fast as possible at the old wreck, pull up with a squeal of the motor and scream of tyres.

As he did so, Lillee and a couple of the others were out of the bus peering at the 'damage' to the jalopy and of course berating our driver for his 'carelessness'.

This display caused the driver to laugh until the tears ran down his cheeks and he was laughing all the harder when out of the jalopy stepped two nuns in full regalia.

Suddenly the humour of the affair had disappeared for our man Lillee—and we saw no more of his favourite trick for quite a while.

One night however he decided it was about time for a comeback. We were attending another of those tedious official functions that cricketers around the world have to endure. Cricketers, like most sportsmen on tour, get a bit blasé about these functions.

But the setting for this party was extraordinary. We drove in through an enormous, white ornate gateway and along a driveway that seemed to stretch for a mile. The house—more like a palace—was fronted with Corinthian columns and a huge flight of white marble steps led up to a doorway even more ornate than the gates. Inside were vaulted ceilings towering twenty feet above us, and the function was held in a ballroom that might well have featured in a Hollywood musical extravaganza.

As usual there were servants moving among the guests with paper-thin sardine sandwiches curled up at the edges and the drink was flowing like the Amazon.

But we were hungry and a group of us—team manager Bill Jacobs, Dennis Lillee, Greg Chappell, Kerry O'Keeffe, and myself decided to take up an invitation from the Australian Trade Commissioner for a few drinks and some good Aussie pies and sauce at his residence.

Our transport that night happened to be a company operating under the name of Taboo Taxis.

We woke the driver from his slumber and gave him directions to the Trade Commissioner's house. As we approached the two white stone pillars of the gateway D. K. Lillee made his play.

He put his arm out of the window and gave the outside of the door a very heavy thump. Then he turned poker-faced and told the startled driver, 'Look what you've done—you've run over the President's dog.'

Quickly the fast bowler was out bending over the front wheel yowling for all the world like a dying dog. The noises were realistically blood-curdling. Lillee, shielded by the darkness kept up the mimicry. Then he carried the 'body' over to the culvert as the 'dog' gave its last gasp.

Lillee returned brushing down his jumper and complaining about the bloodstains. Greg Chappell intervened with his voice very serious too. 'You'll have to go back and tell the President what you've done to his dog.'

'I can't do that man,' the driver wailed. 'I've got a wife and six kids.'

'Then let's get the hell out of here,' Lillee suggested.

We shot out on to the main road which must have been all of twenty feet wide and were making good time when Lillee struck again.

'Watch out for that dog!' he shouted.

There was a wild screech of brakes, the cab slewed sideways and the driver sat there quivering. 'Hey, man, I didn't see nothing,' he moaned.

'You didn't?' Lillee sounded incredulous. 'It was a big black one. He ran right across the road in front of you. You only missed him by an inch.'

Twice more in the next couple of miles there was a re-enactment of the scene. Lillee yelling, car slewing, driver perspiring and near to the point of collapse. After the third incident we proceeded at a much more cautious pace and as luck would have it, the first lamp post we came to had a black-and-white spotted dog sitting at its base.

About 200 yards from the only post the driver dropped right through the gears back to first and crawled along at about half a mile an hour, all the time watching the dog for all he was worth.

Once past, he accelerated like a rocket into the

night. The problem now was we had driven the driver into such a state of shock he was thoroughly lost. We had no idea of where we should be heading. We talked him into stopping at a run-down shanty shop to seek directions.

As we slowed down, a very old grey-haired fellow was alighting from an equally old push bike. The old bloke propped it up on the kerb as our cab pulled in close behind.

Lillee gave the outside of the door a further clout and lo and behold the bike fell over of its own accord!

Dennis was immediately out of the car pretending to push the rear wheel of the bike back into shape watched by the old gentleman whose eyes were standing out like light globes.

Inside the cab the driver was getting a real bawling out, 'You've hit the bloke's bike. It'll cost a fortune to fix. Are you drivers all blind?'

At that moment another car arrived on the scene. By sheer coincidence it was the Trade Commissioner. He stopped abruptly with puzzlement all over his face.

Bill Jacobs was quickly over to the other car explaining our little game to the Trade Commissioner. He immediately entered into the spirit of the affair. He strode around to the front of the cab peered into the window and said: 'I want to see your licence, driver.'

The driver was in an absolute panic. He turned out his pockets, emptied the glove box . . . but no licence.

All the while he was telling the commissioner how poor he was, and how he had to support twelve children (amazing how the number doubled in half an hour!), not to mention what a law abiding citizen he was.

The commissioner began to lecture the poor fellow on the seriousness of knocking down bicycles, but presumably he was getting as peckish as we were, because he brought the show to an end by instructing our driver to follow his car to the 'station', where the matter would be more fully investigated.

He then led the way to his palatial home on a hill

overlooking the city. There the driver received another lecture and the commissioner mentioned that another matter had come to his attention—that of the President's dog. This brought forth a torrent of apologies from the hapless driver and a promise that nothing like it would ever happen again.

The poor fellow was then sent on his way but his ordeal was not over yet because the house was in a narrow dead-end street, and the cab had to go to the end, do a three-point turn and then come back past us.

Never one to let any opportunity slip by, Dennis grabbed hold of a lemon from a nearby tree and as the cab drew level, he let fly scoring a direct hit on the front mudguard.

For a fraction of a second the brakes were applied, then the driver stepped on the accelerator and the cab vanished in a whirl of blue smoke.

I don't remember much about the beer and pies, but I'll never forget that cab driver. And I have a suspicion that he'll never forget us!

★ Umpire: Bowling over the wicket or round the wicket, son?

Boy: My dad told me to bowl at the bloody wicket!'

★ Watching Ian Healy's face when his appeal has been turned down for a stumping is like watching a pickpocket when he finds out that there is no bottom in your pocket.

★ Let me tell you what sort of a guy Max Walker really is.

When he goes to a party nobody says 'Hello.'

But when he leaves everybody says 'Goodbye.'

Aussie Rules

★To be a parking inspector a man would have to have the morals of a boundary umpire.

—Lou Richards

★ My father, Big Max, told the story of how he snuck into my schoolground one day, when I was about nine, to see how I was going in a football game. He wasn't that impressed. When I came home, he gave me a real tongue-lashing: 'You stood there all day with your arms crossed and you never made one attempt to go for the ball!'

'Don't go crook on me, Dad,' I said, 'I was only supposed to be the goalpost today!'

★ Ron Barassi made no. 31 a legend. As a super coach Barassi demanded, and got, respect.

Recently he climbed on to the superhighway of technology—and installed a computer in his office. His first question to it was, 'How far does the average player move in a game?'

The computer answered, 'Four thousand.'

Barassi said, 'Four thousand what?'

And the computer said, 'Four thousand, sir.'

★ I realised there are drugs in Aussie Rules the day I saw a player go up for a high ball and didn't come down!

★ Taking your wife on an end-of-season footie trip is like going hunting with a game warden.

★ I once knew a couple who had a terrible row with their children, and disinherited them. Sad really.

Well, they didn't exactly disinherit them . . . what they did was invest all their money in the Fitzroy football club (now merged with the Brisbane Bears).

★ They were going to panel the dressing room with Tasmanian timber but decided against it.

Probably because the club already had too much dead wood.

★ I used to imagine getting my first kick in VFL football somewhere near the members' wing on the MCG, in front of 70,000 screaming fans. The dream was always consistent: the struggle of gaining possession, then the kick!

The kick was the easy part—simply a matter of putting the football, lace-upwards, gently to the ground. You see, drop kicks were my specialty, whereas today they are non-existent. A player would be dragged from the ground by his coach and fined a thousand dollars for even attempting one.

That wasn't the case during my dreams in the 1950s. Nightly, I used to feel the pigskin bag of wind make perfect contact with my highly polished boot. Big Max used to stress, 'Even if you can't play the game, at least look as if you can.' The resultant energy would propel the football spectacularly, end over end, some sixty-five metres onto the half-forward line where a team-mate would stand on an opponent's head to take the 'mark of the day' and goal.

The MCC members' stand would rise 'as one' to applaud. Dressed in their grey, gaberdine overcoats, and with cigar smoke creating a blue grey haze over their heads, they would continue to clap like mad, long after the goal.

It was 1967 when I made my début in senior football for the Melbourne Football Club. With only seven games of the season remaining, I'd finally got my chance—against North Melbourne, at the MCG. I was the last player selected on the supplementary list and consequently given guernsey No. 46. Yours truly was so skinny (twelve stone nine pounds, or about 80 kilos), that the '4' started just under my left armpit, and the '6' finished under my right. As I ran down the race in a short-sleeved jumper, my mid-winter 'tan' could be described as 'polar bear white', and my elbows were extremely pointy.

No. 35—half-back flanker, dashing Don Williams—was playing his two-hundredth game. I was so excited, I didn't know whether the team was lining up in ceremony for his two-hundredth or my first! I charged through the large red-and-blue banner and jogged a couple of laps on pure adrenalin to soak up the atmosphere. It was magnificent, until seconds before the start of the contest . . . There I stood, in the middle of the fabulous Melbourne Cricket Ground. The umpire held the ball aloft in one hand and drew the tiny stainless steel container to his lips with the other.

Then I noticed the guy standing opposite me in the blue-and-white striped jumper—Noel Teasdale—a giant, barrel-chested man of almost seventeen stone (108 kilograms). On his forehead he wore a leather patch which protected a metal plate inside his skull, the legacy of an old wound.

One team-mate suggested it was to hold his brains intact.

Off went the siren, down went the ball and around went the pea in the whistle.

It should be understood that, at eighteen years of age, Maxwell Henry Norman Walker was a willowy, high-leapin' young fella from the Apple Isle. With eyes firmly fixed on the ball, I charged at the centre circle and leapt high in the air for the knockout, so high in fact that a copper on the boundary line later tried to book me for 'loitering in the air'! Unfortunately it wasn't high enough!

At precisely the same moment as when my fist made contact with the footy, Teasdale's huge frame crashed into mine with catastrophic results. He punched the ball about forty metres towards his goal, and sent No. 46 for the Demons about twenty-five metres in the same direction.

There I was, spread-eagled lying flat on my back and gasping in the middle of the MCG, with not an ounce of wind in my lungs, wondering what in the bloody hell had hit me! But nothing in the world beats perseverance, so I persevered.

Five minutes of the quarter had elapsed when the

ball carried over the boundary line, in front of the smokers' grandstand, on the wing for a throw-in. I then remembered what the legendary coach, Norm Smith, had told me before the game: 'You're a big kid, son. Get in front. Make them climb over you!'

I followed his advice. Immediately, I used my edge in natural pace to gain front position and knock the pill down to rover and captain Hassa Mann, who had a baulk, a weave and a bounce or two before dobbing a magnificent goal on the run.

At this stage I thought to myself, 'How long has this game been going on? You little beauty!' and headed back to the centre circle for the bounce-up. Teasdale jogged level with me and whispered bluntly, 'If you get in front once more, son, I'll knock your so-and-so head right off your shoulder blades!' (And I've cleaned that line up quite considerably here!)

Now, why should I take any notice of this gorilla with the bondage head-gear? I'd heard similar comments from other players, all to no avail. Without thinking too much about his threat, I later prepared to contest another boundary throw—on the members' wing again.

No worries, I easily gained front position. I placed my hand on the ball beautifully to palm it down to No. 29, Hassa . . . but then it happened. Whack!—right in the back of the neck. I pulled up centimetres inside the white boundary line, my chin firmly implanted in the moist turf.

'Play on!' was the call by the umpire.

'Gee, a bloke can be stiff,' I thought, 'no free kick.' Remember, too, I hadn't got my first kick in VFL football yet! But Lady Luck definitely wasn't smiling on me at all . . . the footy had trickled awkwardly only 20 metres further on, before rolling over the line and out of bounds!

I explored the possibility of continuing to take front position. Then, instead, I decided to attempt to nudge the ball out to nippy winger Stanley Alves (current coach of St. Kilda Football Club) at the back of the pack. And it would've been great . . . but little did I realise that 'Teaser' had no time for the subtleties of the game. This time he unloaded me with a 'coat hanger' (elbow) behind the left ear! Down I went like a bag of wet cement, church bells ringing loudly inside my head. Seconds later the umpire nearly burst my right ear-drum by bending down, blowing the whistle, and announcing he was awarding me a free kick!

Like a flash, out came Sam Alicia, the MFC runner. 'Kick it, kick it, quick!' he roared. He must have thought I was Superman—my legs had completely buckled under me. Sam's strong hands, under each armpit, supported me. A kick was still out of the question. Maybe a handball?

Suddenly, Sam dug deep into his white cricket-trouser pocket. As is the case with trainers who've been around a while, Sammy had a small packet of 'smelling salts' for such an occasion. The top was off the packet in a hurry, and under my nose it was jammed. The smell was terrible, nevertheless it made my eyes water and head spin, and my subsequent handball did reach a Melbourne player nearby. I was beginning to wonder whether or not I was ever going to get a kick.

While recovering in the back pocket, my dream became a reality. At the eleven-minute mark of the first quarter, I attacked the ball as it was kicked across the half-back line. The pill was about to bounce about two metres in front of me. Which way would the egg-shaped ball bounce? Fortunately for me, it hit me fair and square on the left nipple! Here was my big chance!

There it was, safe in my possession., I held it at arm's length and looked: MATCH II, Tom Sherrin, Rawhide Leather, Made in Australia. The real thing! You little ripper!

Now for the kick, blue-and-white vertical striped jumpers everywhere. Not much time. Unlike in the technicolour dream created in the computer between my ears, this memorable first kick was a wobbly old flat punt that travelled only thirty-five metres.

Whatever it looked like, I'll remember that kick for the rest of my days, simply because it was my FIRST!

★ Who among us has not stood on the outer, looked at our local team playing and said, 'I must be out of my mind, watching this lot.'

★ The ground announcer before the game: 'Today's game is being televised and sent to our soldiers overseas, which is the government's way of saying that the people back home are not having such a good time either.'

★ They were forming a new club and the first speaker said, 'Liars, cheats and know-alls will not be allowed on our club board.'

The second speaker said, 'You'd better strike out know-alls or you'll never get a quorum.'

★ The office was due to open at 9 a.m. and the queue for the Grand Final tickets was three blocks long.

Murphy strode to the top of the queue.

The giant who stood there threw Murphy to the ground.

Three times he got up—three times he was thrown to the ground.

Finally he said, 'You throw me to the ground one more time and as God is my judge, I'm never going to unlock that office door.'

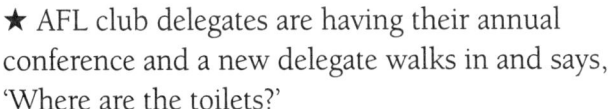

★ AFL club delegates are having their annual conference and a new delegate walks in and says, 'Where are the toilets?'

And Newton who has attended many conferences says, 'Son, there are no toilets here. Everybody shits on everybody else.'

★ 'We all ought to be certified for getting back into this bastard of a plane!' shouted Sam Newman from the rear of our temporary prison. For surely, we were doing time the hard way—trapped in a tiny flying machine.

Sam, the former Geelong VFL footballer and now a multi-media mega star, was sharing the second, or back row, of a four-seater, twin-engine Cessna next to notorious Melbourne television character, Peter 'Crackers' Keenan, a veteran of more than 250 games with VFL clubs Melbourne, North Melbourne and Essendon. Today he is a member of the much respected ABC radio commentary team.

Yours truly was in the cramped cockpit—in the seat reserved for the co-pilot. From the beginning, I had been almost hypnotised by the glaring mass of illuminated green and yellow gauges before my eyes.

Graeme, our young pilot, was responsible for safely transporting Sam, Crackers and myself to and from a speaking engagement in the small town of Cohuna, in the north of Victoria.

The aircraft was being buffeted continually, like a

lost balloon, in strong wind gusts. The plane had just fallen abruptly—about 1000 feet—when Sam said, 'Gee, I feel close to God, but I don't want to meet him just yet!'

I've got it on pretty good authority that there was some good money within the four of us to suggest that we would not make it back to ground in one piece! And I'm not telling any lies when I say we were very bloody frightened. Maybe it was the bad beginning to our epic journey?

What a way to start! As we calmly taxied down the black bitumen tarmac, there was very little discussion, other than the preceding week's events. At near top speed, our wheels left the tarmac of Essendon airport.

A perfect take-off I thought. Sammy and Crackers didn't really care as they dissected VFL footballers' recent performances. Whatever the field, old players never die, they just become experts in their sport.

'Bloody hell!' Sam screamed, as we were barely 300 feet above the ground, and still climbing. The pilot's door flew open. Wind at about 160 kmh gushed into the cockpit. My heart began pounding very loudly—I was terrified! And I know that I wasn't an orphan in feeling like that!

I flung my left arm across the pilot's back, like any 'great' slips fieldsman might, to grab the flapping door. Simultaneously, both hands from the 6'4" ruckman from Geelong appeared from the other direction, desperately trying to pull the door shut.

Crackers was issuing the obvious instruction at the top of his voice: 'Shut the bloody door, quick shut it, c'mon Sam shut it!'

The door would not close, despite superhuman efforts by Sam and myself.

Through all this, the pilot was huddled grim-faced over the aeroplane's controls to give us a better chance to slam the door.

The lights of Essendon were all too bright below us—barely 200 metres off the ground. For some reason, the door still would not slam shut after several more vigorous attempts. Graeme struggled with the joystick as we banked steeply round the control tower.

At one stage, I reckon we must have been flying sideways at ninety degrees to Earth and hanging on for grim death. I felt the long legs of Peter Pius Paul Keenan almost pushed through the back of my seat as he fought the forces of gravity.

A unanimous decision was made to land the plane and find out what was wrong—who said footballers had no brains? On this occasion, common-sense prevailed!

I had visions of someone—hopefully not me—being sucked out the open door into the cold dark night air, never to be seen again! Did you ever see the film *Airport '75*?

The very large lump in my throat had moved and lodged somewhere near the back of my ears as we levelled out over the Tullamarine freeway . . . if only we can land this plane safely?

I should not have doubted Graeme's ability, for the Cessna came in for a smooth landing. The 'team' was right back where we started five minutes earlier.

Nerves frayed, but confidence restored, we powered down the runway for the second time. Crackers suggested that the air traffic controller in the tower probably thought he was drunk, seeing the same plane take off twice in seven minutes. But it didn't last long as we struggled into very strong headwinds. We should have been travelling at 160 knots, instead we were averaging only 105.

Long before we reached Bendigo, we agreed that it was the worst flight we had ever been on, except for Graeme, who was showing a brave face.

Then the small charter plane pressed forward relentlessly into the face of a very nasty storm. Visibility could have been barely ten metres—we truly were flying blind.

Graeme would not dare let his hands leave the controls as we continually dropped out of the sky with devastating effects on my stomach, which had become horribly knotted.

We were told that sick bags were in the seat pockets. I was too scared to be sick . . . Crackers said that if he was going to be sick, then it was only

right the pilot should wear it. From where I sat . . .
it was odds on that I would wear it.

I should mention too that Crackers had been out
to lunch: and garlic prawns had been on the menu.
Every time he opened his mouth it suggested an
Indian flame thrower at work . . . and the plane's
interior was beginning to smell like an oven full of
garlic bread.

My palms were very sweaty, and I'm certain that
the giant ruckmen behind were holding hands as we
plummeted through the clouds.

The rain on the wings now looked like huge
sparks illuminated by the flashing wing lights—
heavy drops were pounding on the windscreen.

I never have felt so insecure for such a long
period of time! The two lads in the back were joking
nervously about the possible news stories if we went
down.

Something along the line of: 'Football will miss
Peter Keenan and Sam Newman, the two VFL
champion footballers tragically killed with their
friend, former Test cricketer Max Walker, when their

light aircraft crashed north of Bendigo last night on its way to a speaking engagement at Cohuna.'

I don't think our pilot was impressed. But I'm sure he realised our grave situation. As Crackers said: 'Don't worry Maxie, he's a mature twenty one-year-old.'

I thought here we are, our lives in the hands of a fragile, metal machine with two props and a twenty one-year-old pilot. Unreal, and for what? A few hundred dollars for the night.

Sam said: 'How far is it to Cohuna, one and a half hours? We've been going for one and a half hours and haven't looked like sighting bloody Cohuna!'

'Yeah,' Crackers said impatiently, 'we should've driven up—could have saved a few bob and a lot of heartache!'

Finally, almost two hours after our original take-off, we were in the vicinity of our flight destination, Kerang. We were flying at about 1500 metres, give or take a thousand feet depending on the clouds and rain. All we had to do was find the airstrip.

I watched the altimeter spin from 1600 metres to

well below 300 metres—still no sign of the strip. My ears popped and I hung on tight, hoping there was no radio tower or mountain tucked away secretly in the darkness below us.

Then, from nowhere, the two parallel blue lines appeared to our right—I didn't think that two blue lines could ever look so good. We did one arbitrary lap of honour before we made our final approach to land.

The nervous tension had got to us—we all started laughing as Graeme again put us on deck with a beautiful landing in pouring rain.

While the propellors unwound, and our aeroplane came to a stand-still. I thought: no way am I getting back into this kite, unless we've got clear skies. Judging by the amount of water bouncing off the wings it looked like overnight at Cohuna.

You are not going to believe me when I tell you this, but about 12.30 a.m. we left Kerang in clear skies. But around Bendigo we hit the storms again and sat through the same fear for another hour.

We could not get Graeme to admit that it was the worst flying conditions he had flown in. But he did describe them 'as a long way from the best'.

I can understand why people hate small aircraft or flying full stop—you feel so helpless! Never again!

★ Michael was the parish priest at St Kilda, and a passionate follower of St Kilda, so when one of his parishioners, who was a Collingwood supporter, died, the relations approached him nervously. The Saints beat the Magpies by a point to win the '66 flag.

'Would you refuse to bury a Collingwood supporter?'

'Refuse? Of course not. I just wish I could be burying them all day,' he grinned.

★ The players are stripping off in the dressing room when one player turns to the new Aboriginal player and says, 'What are those things around your neck—human teeth?'

'No, alligator teeth,' he replied proudly.

'I see,' said the player very patronisingly, 'I suppose they have the same value to your people as pearls have to us white people.'

'Not quite,' said the Aborigine. 'Anyone can open an oyster.'

★ As the Footscray club president said around contract time: 'I have the greatest respect for our coach. I worship the quicksand he walks on.'

★ The club president and talent scout had toured the breadth of the country searching for new players. When the president returned he met the coach.

'How did you do?' asked the coach.

'Well, we saw one team with fifteen straight wins and averaging 120 points a game. But the funny thing is, they were mostly under 60 kg in weight and any of them that were over 5 ft 6 in were over 40 years of age.'

'Well,' said the coach, 'I don't suppose you signed any of them?'

'No,' said the president, 'but I did sign their coach as your successor.'

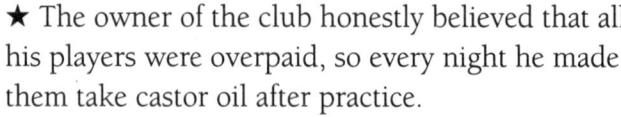

★ The owner of the club honestly believed that all his players were overpaid, so every night he made them take castor oil after practice.

He said he knew it didn't make them better players, but at least he felt they were now giving him a better run for his money.

★ It was the same owner who made the player a million-dollar offer—a dollar a year for a million years.

★ I think 'Captain Blood' Jack Dyer, the rough and tough Richmond ruckman was spot-on when he told me: 'That Lou Richards was so ugly as a four-year-old kid, his mum used to have to hang the lamb chops around his neck to get their dog to play with him.'

★ A gunman goes into the Fitzroy Football Club social club and says, 'Give me everything you have.'

The treasurer says, 'How do you want it—heads or tails?'

★ It was a tough club. The leader of the cheergirls was a granite-faced Charles Bronson. The club mascot was a piranha . . . with this club you didn't sign a contract, you signed a will!

★ The Carlton Football Club has so much money it is the only football club to have a sauna with air-conditioning. The opposition . . . well, they regularly have to put up with rusty plumbing and cold showers.

★ The coaches have been speaking for over an hour, and one of the slightly deaf players said to his mate, 'Has he finished yet?'

'Yeah,' says his mate, 'but he hasn't stopped.'

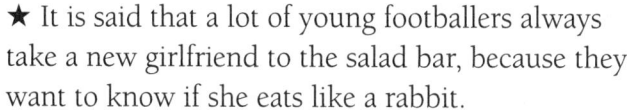

★ It is said that a lot of young footballers always take a new girlfriend to the salad bar, because they want to know if she eats like a rabbit.

★ With all the money he earned from football, television and commercials, he bought a typical bachelor's apartment.

High fidelity in one corner, infidelity in the other.

★ His bachelor apartment was a wild life sanctuary.

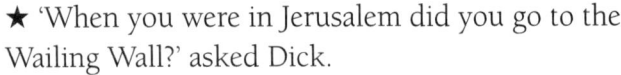

★ 'When you were in Jerusalem did you go to the Wailing Wall?' asked Dick.

'Yes, I did, but I couldn't get near it for Collingwood supporters.'

★ 'You really are an extraordinary man,' stated the interviewer on *Wide World of Sports*, 'boxing champion at 66 years of age.'

'Heck, I'm not as good as my dad. He's 88 and he's just signed to play in the back pocket for Richmond. He's in Perth now at his father's wedding and he's 114,' replied the guest.

'Absolutely amazing—you're a boxing champion at 66, your father's a footballer at 88, and your grandfather wants to get married at 114?'

'Hey, grandad doesn't want to get married . . . he has to get married!'

★ Wayne couldn't play last weekend, because he got injured fighting for his girlfriend's honour.

She wanted to keep it!

★ Inside the medical room:

'I'm a bit worried. The doc has put me on a diet and it's made me so horny that last night I bit my girlfriend's ear,' explains the youngster to his team-mate.

'Don't worry', said his mate, 'it's only 30 to 40 calories.'

★ 'I have some good news and some bad news,' he told the assembled players.

'The bad news is that the club is going broke and cannot honour your contracts. As your Players Association representative, I have agreed with management that all players will agree to a 40 per cent reduction in salary.

'The good news is, the management has agreed to backdate this for 12 months.'

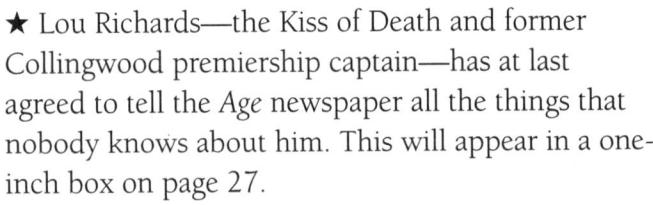

★ Lou Richards—the Kiss of Death and former Collingwood premiership captain—has at last agreed to tell the *Age* newspaper all the things that nobody knows about him. This will appear in a one-inch box on page 27.

★ Lou Richards is the only commentator who has a bracelet on his wrist which reads 'In case of an emergency please call a press conference'.

Sam Newman's bracelet reads: 'In case of an emergency get me a girl'.

★ After watching a troupe of female body builders complete their routines for the Miss Olympia title one morning on *Wide World of Sports—Sunday Edition*, I asked Lou a simple straightforward question in back-announcing the segment: 'What did you think of Dianne—the one in the orange bikini?' She was the contestant he fancied!

After one more squinted look at our TV monitor, Lou let loose with a rip snorter of a reply: 'She'd be pretty handy on a half-back flank for Collingwood wouldn't she?'

Needless to say we had about a hundred letters about his tactless quip . . . but at the time

Collingwood weren't winning too many games and he probably meant it.

★ How a dream can turn into a nightmare: he takes a magnificent pass. He looks around, cannot see any of his team mates ahead, so he runs faster than he ever has, showing amazing agility with the ball.

From 40 metres out, in what appears to be an impossible angle, he boots the ball between the big posts.

He turns around to acknowledge the cheers of the crowd and then and only then he realises he has run the wrong way.

★ During a particularly nasty local derby bottles were flying at an alarming rate. One old digger turned to the young man next to him and said, 'Son there is no need to worry, it's just like what they used to say in the war—if it's got your name on it— it's got your name on it.'

Second spectator says, 'That may be all right for you, but my name is Jack Daniels.'

★ I'm against all forms of terrorism, bombing, hijacking, kidnapping and Lou Richards with a microphone. (Bless you Lou, you are a national treasure.)

★ He stood five foot nothing, weighed 60 kg ringing wet, but was nevertheless a clever coach. In the first meeting with the players he said, 'I have two questions. Is there anyone here who thinks he can whip me?'

Silence prevailed.

Eventually a guy stands up at the back of the room: 6 foot 6, 19 stone—living proof that Darwin was right. 'I think I can whip you,' he said.

'Right,' said the coach and turned to the players. 'Have you met your new captain?'

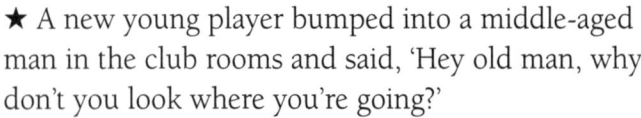

★ The unpopular coach was screaming abuse at his players when one of the club supporters jumped the fence and hit the coach straight in the face.

Next day's headline: 'Trouble at ground when the fan hits the shit.'

★ A new young player bumped into a middle-aged man in the club rooms and said, 'Hey old man, why don't you look where you're going?'

The man replied, 'Look here, sonny, you are talking to the club coach.'

And the kid said, 'I'm sorry, coach. I thought you were only the club President.'

★ Gay footballer: he was a real man's man.

★ He's called before the AFL tribunal charged with striking and elects to defend himself.

'Don't you want legal representation?' asks the chairman.

'No, sir.'

'You are quite certain?'

'If it's all the same to you, I would like to throw myself on the ignorance of the court.'

★ The Fitzroy Football Club were making a TV doco to be called 'The Best of 1991–96'. We think it will run the same time as the commercial.

★ At the completion of my District Cricket segment on HSV 7, Louie stood next to the camera, legs slightly astride, arms high with a huge sheet of butcher's paper. In the corner of his mouth his cigarette began to glow a bright red as he inhaled quickly. His mischievous eyes were dancing left and right looking for attention . . . he had all the support he needed.

My old architecture lecturer, Ron Centre, at the Royal Melbourne Institute of Technology, would have been proud of the lovely lettering on the beige coloured butcher's paper. This graduate from Collingwood Tech had obviously sat down with a chunky felt pen and neatly written my closing message.

What a lovely gesture, I thought, as I began to read, word perfect: 'Well, that just about wraps up the District Cricket . . .'

I never did make it to the end of line two because, quick as a flash, Lou had dug deep into his Christian Dior trouser pocket and produced a cigarette lighter. No ordinary lighter either—a Dunhill, thank you very much! A sure sign the boy from the back streets of Collingwood had a few bob to spend on himself. Well, he doesn't spend it on anyone else!

What do you reckon he did with the tiny gold-plated flame-thrower! You guessed it! He licked the bottom two corners of the paper sign with the flame . . . everyone fell about laughing as I strained to concentrate on my line. Within seconds, the bottom half of the script was going up in smoke and Louie began to cough loudly.

★ It was the annual report of the AGM and the president stood up and said, 'As you know, we always try to help a club that is less successful than ours, but each year they are becoming harder to find.'

★ Things happen very quickly in football.
  'I coach St Kilda.'
  'Oh, did you?'

★ A good sport is one who will always let you have your way.

★ Ross was walking into the footy club one day and as he he gets to the storage room he hears a ghostly voice saying, 'Bring me a horse, bring me a horse.'

The same thing happens for the next three days, so he reports it to the vice-president and they both go down to investigate.

This time the voice said, 'You idiot! I asked you to bring me a horse and you've brought me an ass.'

★ The usual bragging was going on in the dressing room after the game.

The first player said, 'I have a wife who meets me every night at the door and we've been married four years.'

The second player said, 'Well, I have a wife who meets me every night at the station and we've been married thirteen years.'

The third player says, 'I have a wife who meets me every night at a motel and we're not even married.'

★ Club President John Elliott reckons that at the Carlton Football Club they do everything big. At the annual dinner instead of a finger bowl you take a bath.

★ It was a very poor club. After the game someone dropped the towel and it broke.

★ He was a star player who loved the bright lights of the city, so much so that the coach insisted he move to the country. After a few months he is asked about his country lifestyle.

He said, 'It's nice. It's peaceful and quiet. I'm at one with nature. But it has some things against it.'

The interviewer asked, 'What do you miss most?'

He answered, 'The last train home at night.'

★ Nowadays female journalists can enter dressing rooms straight after a game of football.

What bothers players most is when they walk in carrying a measuring tape.

★ A football fan is a person who screams at a player for not being able to pass the ball to his team mate 60 metres away on the blind side of the field. And then, after the game, can't find his own car in the car park.

★ 'You have two tickets. Can I buy one for $150?'

'No way, I'm going to go to that game. Have a few drinks, and scream abuse at the umpire, then I'm going to have a few more drinks and question the parentage of every one in the opposition. Then I'm going to have a few more drinks and probably start a fight, after which if it's like last year, they'll throw me out of the ground. You see. . . then I'm going to need this extra ticket to get back in!' he explained.

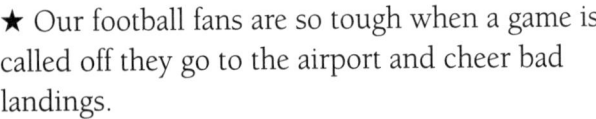

★ 'I hear your husband is in hospital. What happened?'

She replied to her friend, 'Knee trouble.'

'Oh, a football injury?'

'No, I found his young lady friend sitting on it!'

★ Our football fans are so tough when a game is called off they go to the airport and cheer bad landings.

★ Perhaps I was guilty of neglecting my feet at the expense of the fluff on my face. The result was an in-grown toe nail. Precisely what I didn't need at the beginning of the 1967 VFL season with so much fitness work and kicking of the football to do.

Yes, it did hurt to kick! My big toe hurt a lot. It even hurt to put my street shoes on . . . thongs were more the order of the day!

Consequently I fronted up to practice one cold and wet Tuesday night in April hoping not to have to train. I walked into the medical room only metres past the numbered, grey metal lockers in the Melbourne Football Club's dressing room at the Melbourne Cricket Ground.

The first person I ran into was our medico, Bob Ashbey, who took one look and referred me immediately to our physiotherapist at the time. The Demons used to go through them like half-back flankers!

After asking the educated man if it was possible to give me a couple of pills to fix up my badly festered toe, he said, 'The medical profession has come a long way but unfortunately for you, son—not that far!'

He confirmed my worst thoughts—there was no pill in the world capable of fixing an inflamed and badly infected in-grown toe nail!

Confront the problem like a man, I kept telling myself. My confrontation with Dr Colin Galbraith, the MFC club doctor, turned out to be pretty horrific. After exchanging the normal pleasantries in the consulting rooms at the rear of his house, we settled down to the business of a remedy.

Soon I was sitting on a very low stool, exposing my right foot for him to inspect. Expecting the worst, I was naturally on edge, and when he grabbed my big toe in his right hand it was like levitation—I rose about half a metre vertically off the stool in response to the acute pain!

Doctors sometimes suggest they have to be cruel to be kind—well they're not wrong! When he let go of my foot, the doctor said in a jovial manner: 'I've got just the thing to fix this up my boy!'

He walked away to the antique, roll-top desk. All

I could hear and see was what appeared to be re-arranging of papers. When Doc finally turned around, there before my eyes was . . . this huge needle about 15 centimetres long.

Before I could prevent my cold-hearted friend from grabbing my toe again, he had it in a vice-like grip. Then with a great deal of conviction, almost pleasure, the silver haired, bespectacled doctor plunged the shiny silver needle deep into the heart of my much throbbing toe—the pain was excruciating to say the least and this was supposed to be a pain-killing injection. I wanted to shout, but no sound came forth . . . like a goldfish.

Next he opted for a second dash at the action. This time he drove the painkiller into the top of the rather red big toe. At this stage, not only was a yellow looking liquid seeping from the edge of the toe-nail, but my eyes were also beginning to well with moisture.

I almost blacked out when the third and final jab scored a direct hit below the toe.

It seemed like eternity before the toe 'deadened'.

Now for the real heavy stuff! The doctor began to cut out the offending piece of jagged nail from deep in the edge of my big toe. I was still conscious . . . surgical scissors performing their task—a precise cut was made parallel to the edge of my toe. Then a change of instrument—a pair of right angled scissors were produced. Blood was freely flowing from the wound, despite the lack of feeling, I didn't like it!

The good doctor continued the 'operation' with a right-angled cut—this was too much! I fainted and fell face first towards the floor.

★ Laurie Dwyer, the former North Melbourne star used to give his cattle human names.

He reckoned that at one stage his herd consisted of every club president in Melbourne.

★ 'Your Honour, I know I was speeding. But, gee . . . I was only trying to get to the club for training on time,' Kevin pleaded.

'Did you make it?' the judge asked.

'Yes,' Kev beamed.

'Who do you play for?'

'Richmond.'

'Case dismissed. This man has been punished enough!'

★ Sledging opposition players in order to put them off their game has become a regular part of sport. Ever since Eve scored and Adam converted.

This is strictly so in Aussie rules, where a player's parentage is constantly being questioned, where behind play you are likely to hear voices telling you that your mother doesn't go to bingo on a Tuesday night because she works in a house of ill repute.

My favourite is attributed to Crackers Keenan, who said to his opposite number: 'You are the greatest idiot in the game. In fact, if they were having a contest to find out who was the biggest idiot in the world you'd run second.'

His opponent answered, 'Why would I run second?'

Crackers replied, 'Because you are such an idiot.'

★ The late Mr Football Ted Whitten on Sam Newman, former Geelong ruckman and *Footy Show*'s top gun.

'I've been checking out your family tree, Sam.'

'And . . .?'

'All I could find was one cactus after another . . . I've never seen so many pricks in my entire life!'

★ Ted Whitten, explaining why Sam—the 50-year-old playboy with a fancy for younger women—was late for the start of the *Sunday Footy Show*.

'. . . You were seen standing outside the Women's Hospital waiting for your next wife to be born!'

★ My team-mate, Peter 'Crackers' Keenan, had managed to get his nose broken earlier one afternoon while playing football—it was a bitter brawling encounter between our team, Melbourne, and Essendon.

Judging by the swelling and the exaggerated kink in Crackers' more than ample nose, Essendon not only won the match, but they also won the fight!

Nevertheless, our weekly after-match ritual of getting together was now well underway—win, lose or draw, it was always good for team spirit and morale.

Honestly, Crackers Keenan is not a handsome

man. In fact I'm sure his head was chiselled out of granite—now his busted beak didn't help the image.

Sitting opposite the huge, macho ruckman was the wife of one of Melbourne's most respected businessmen.

The businessman's blue Rolls Royce was parked outside the restaurant and his other half was dressed in splendour—blue-rinse hairdo, bright red lipstick, enormous diamond sparklers hanging from each ear-lobe and several dead foxes draped across her pale shoulders.

The beautifully manicured lady couldn't help but notice the three rapidly expanding blobs of blood in my mate's bowl!

But cool as an ice-cube, the big fella looked up, straight across the table, took a deep breath through his partly blocked nose—to stem the flow of blood without having to use his handkerchief—then confidently plunged his silver spoon deep into the heart of his soup.

At the same time the elegant lady's cheeks became ashen-grey. Yes, she'd guessed it. Crackers was going to eat it—blood and all. How could he? There he was Peter Pius Paul Keenan, fresh from the famous Catholic college at Kilmore Assumption— dressed in a 'closing down' sale, purple polyester suit, pink shirt, wide paisley tie matching his even wider lapels, white socks and an outrageous pair of black pointy-toed shoes. It was clear to see our man was right at the forefront of early seventies fashion, even though he was sitting on his tastebuds.

Within seconds he'd swallowed his first spoonful of blood-stained soup, with much disgust all round—it really was a sickening sight.

His 'friend' across the soup bowl, waited only three more spoonfuls before leaving the party . . . but as Crackers said, 'Where's she gone, the night's only just begun?'

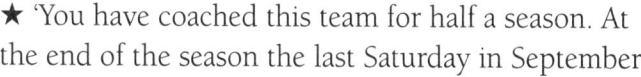

★ 'You have coached this team for half a season. At the end of the season the last Saturday in September the final siren blows at the MCG, 100,000 fans go mad, your team Collingwood have just won the flag. What do you say to the Collingwood fans?'

'Nothing.'

'What would you say to the players?'

'Nothing.'

'On an occasion like that you just wouldn't say anything to anybody?'

'Well, I couldn't. I'd be dead from the shock.' (Collingwood won in '58 and '90.)

★ The days of my youth when I'd come home with bloody knee, torn clothes, my shoes covered in mud, and my mum would say, 'Brian, you've been playing football with those rough boys from down the street.'

And I'd say, 'No mum, they've been playing football with me.'

★ North Melbourne fan discussing the Swan legend, Tony Lockett.

'I tell you what's wrong with Plugger. I admit that he can kick, he can pass and he's tough. But when he doesn't have possession of the ball he does nothing.'

'You are quite right. You have discovered his fatal weakness—he can't score without the ball.'

'But how do you keep it off him?'

★ Years ago the best present you could give the St Kilda players was a cigarette lighter because they kept losing their matches.

★ Sam Newman once said, 'I must be walking in my sleep, this morning I woke up in my own bed.'

★ Warwick Capper was granted an audience with
the Pope. He shakes the Pope's hand and says,
'You're looking well, how's your dear lady wife, your
holiness?'

There was an embarrassing silence when
someone whispered in Warwick's ear, 'The Pope is
not allowed to marry.'

'Well all right,' said Warwick, 'how was I to
know? Nobody's infallible.'

★ Some players' egos are greater than their
footballing ability, to say the least.

He was the king of ego. On their first date he
bragged heaps about his achievements both on and
off the field. He spoke so much about himself that
even he realised that he was losing her.

Finally, he said, 'I've spoken so much about
myself, let's talk about you. Tell me, how do you
think I played last Saturday?'

★ When he retires it will still be considered a great career move.

★ A true football fan in Melbourne only pays half-price admission because he only watches one team!

★ The night before the Grand Final the Catholic coach sent all of his players to church to light a candle.

Then they stayed up all night making sure that the other team didn't come and blow it out.

★ The coach, like a lot of modern coaches banned the players from having sex for a week before the

Grand Final, on the grounds that it tires them out. However, on the night before, he returns to the hotel to find his star player indulging in what can only be called Mummies and Daddies.

'Harry,' said the coach, 'I am both shocked and disappointed. The night before the Grand Final, despite all that I have told you about conserving your energy, I find you in this position. You are letting me down. You are letting yourself down, letting your team mates down . . .

'Harry, Harry! Could you please stop while I'm talking to you?'

★ A well-known Melbourne identity who is known for his intelligent generosity and his love of the St Kilda football club gives the club large cheques.

But he likes to remain anonymous, so he never signs them.

★ The worst thing about playing a great game is that you will be expected to keep up that standard for the rest of the season.

★ So many players today are on incentive payments that being dropped to reserves is like having a stake driven through your wallet.

★ You know your contract is not being renewed when they send the priest to accompany you to the manager's office.

Or when you turn up for training and the club has moved.

★ The voice on the phone says, 'I'd like to talk to the stupid idiot who runs this club.'

The secretary responds, 'How dare you!' and slams down the receiver.

Two minutes later the phone rings again and the same voice says, 'Listen, I'm sorry if I offended you but I have supported this team, man and boy for forty years. I am now a multimillionaire and if you can put me through to the chief executive I would be obliged because I want to donate two million dollars to the club.'

Quick as a flash, the secretary said, 'I'll get the stupid bastard for you right now!'

★ A monologue is a half-time conversation between Ron Barassi and his team.

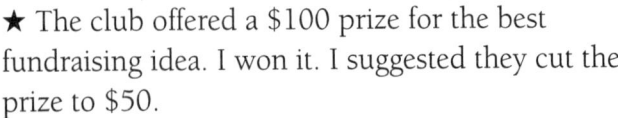

★ The club offered a $100 prize for the best fundraising idea. I won it. I suggested they cut the prize to $50.

★ He called the board of directors 'a bunch of wankers', and got fined for divulging a club secret.

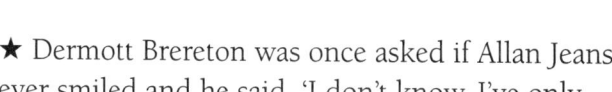

★ Dermott Brereton was once asked if Allan Jeans ever smiled and he said, 'I don't know. I've only known him nine years.'

★ A nice club president: if he likes you he invites you over for a swim in his pool.

If you play well and actually win a game he puts water in the pool.

★ The way Kevin Sheedy believes in himself is very encouraging in these atheistic days, when so many believe in no God at all.

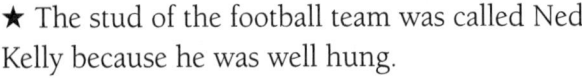

★ Mark was a big-headed player, and like all big-headed players he was troublesome.

He spoke to the coach at the meeting and said, 'Coach, how will I know when it is time to retire?'

The coach said, 'Well, first, you'll see the smile on my face.'

★ The expression 'love at first sight' was probably invented by a player on an end-of-season trip.

★ The stud of the football team was called Ned Kelly because he was well hung.

★ They called him 'Cinderella' because he ran away from the ball.

★ They called the Chairman of selectors the 'Oven' because every time he spoke to the players he would give them a bake.

★ They called the coach 'Singlet' because he was on everyone's back.

★ They called the secretary 'Mirror' because he was always promising to look into things.

★ They called the property steward the 'Lid' because he was always topping the story he'd just heard.

★ He arrived at training covered in bruises, black and blue all over. And he was also an hour late. David Parkin started to give him hell.

'But coach,' said the player, 'it wasn't my fault I fell from a five-storey building.'

And Parkin said, 'So what? It didn't take you an hour to do that, did it?'

★ The young kid from the bush arrived at the club. And the chief executive signed him on a monthly trial without salary.

After the month he was so successful, they kept him on at double the salary.

★ Monday morning training after suffering a heavy defeat, the coach of Essendon Kevin Sheedy is addressing the players very angrily, like a plumber in a deep wet trench.

'Listen, some of you players seem to be ignorant of the basic rules of this game. Let me start at the beginning. This is a football, and the object of the game is . . .'

And a voice from the back of the bunch says, 'Hey coach, not so fast.'

He'd have to be a ruckman.

★ The coach was defending his mate to the committee.

'Let me tell you this—as a player he has more talent in his little finger than he has in his big finger.'

★ High in the Great Southern Stand at the MCG, an anti-Collingwood spectator asks, 'What is the difference between a dead Collingwood supporter on the road and a dead pig?'

Obviously the skid marks are in front of the pig!

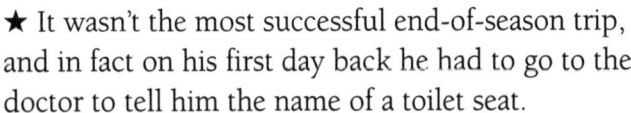

★ It wasn't the most successful end-of-season trip, and in fact on his first day back he had to go to the doctor to tell him the name of a toilet seat.

★ As the experienced player uses the art of gamesmanship and tries to put the young seventeen-year-old off his game.

He says sharply while planting an elbow to the ribcage, 'Does your mother know you're out?'

And the smart kid replies without hesitation,

'She should. I weighed nine pounds at birth!'

Fifteen all.

★ He was crying his eyes out.

'What's wrong, Pat?'

'Oh, I've just seen a coachload of Collingwood supporters go over a cliff.'

'So what are you crying about? You support St Kilda.'

'I know, but there were six empty seats.'

★ He took her to her first game of Australian Rules, and they were standing in the open. It was belting down with rain.

At the end of the first quarter she turned to her loved one and said, 'I know I'm ignorant of the finer points of this game, but would you mind if I asked you one question?'

'Certainly dear, it's nice to know you're interested in the game. What do you want to know?'

'Well,' she said sweetly, 'why can't we bloody well go home?'

★ He was running away from the play, but the ball hit him fair and square on the backside.

The trainer rushed on and said, 'Hey, the coach wants to know if you are OK.'

The player said, 'Why did he ask me that?'

'Well, we thought you might have had a brain concussion!'

★ He is a typical footy supporter. Loves a pie 'n' sauce, loves a beer.

He knows every statistic on every player but only the first two lines of 'Advance Australia Fair'.

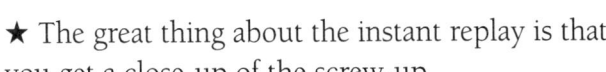

★ The great thing about the instant replay is that you get a close-up of the screw-up.

★ The suburban football team accidentally left all their dirty gear on the bus. Later the local paper ran an ad:

'If the person or persons who left their football gear on the No. 19 bus would care to come down to the bus station, they can have the bus.'

★ Selling merchandise is such a big part of sport today, I know one club that brags they sell a $300 club scarf every four minutes—which is not that great if you think about it, because there is one born every minute.

★ Every vegetable known on the island, and a vast quantity of rotten eggs, were hurled at Big Max and his umpiring colleagues at the end of the footy match. They'd also let all four tyres down on his zappy little army-green 1950 Ford Prefect. Dad simply had to bury his head and cop the lot while he slowly pumped up each tyre.

After another match at Molesworth he was hoisted shoulder-high by players and officials. 'I didn't think I went that well,' a beaming Big Max yelled to the crowd beneath him.

'You didn't. We're going to chuck you in the bloody creek,' said one of the wits in the milling throng.

★ The captain of the Western Bulldogs spent the whole afternoon questioning the umpire's every decision. Eventually the umpire had had enough. He called him over.

'Hey, who is umpiring this game—you or me?'

The captain looked at him with a smile and said, 'Neither of us.' I would think that the Bulldogs lost that game by heaps!

★ Sam Newman has an Errol Flynn reputation, which is not surprising when even he admits his bedroom has an interchange bench. What's more, Sam agrees with Essendon coach Kevin Sheedy in wanting to extend the numbers of interchange players!

★ 'Do you support Collingwood?' asked Sam on the top-rating *Footy Show's* 'Street-talk'.

'I never miss them,' admitted one wearing a black 'n' white beanie.

'That's good,' said Sam.

'Yep . . . I never watch them, and I never miss them!' barked another.

★ They were playing at the Holy Cross school, when one not-too-bright forward began abusing the Pope.

Well after the riot, the team manager took him aside, 'You're a complete and utter idiot! Don't you know the Holy Cross team is Catholic?'

He said, 'I knew that, but I didn't know the Pope was.'

★ 'You love football more than you love me.'

'That's true, but look on the bright side—I love you more than I love cricket.'

★ He went to confession. 'I ran to the other side of the ground and belted an opposing player.'

'That was very wrong, my son,' said the priest, making a chalk mark on his sleeve.

'And Father, when he fell, I kicked him in the groin.'

'That is terrible, my son. You must think of your fellow man,' the priest said, making another chalk mark.

'And Father, when the umpire had his back turned I belted him in the face.'

'Son,' said the priest, making another mark on his sleeve, 'you are a disgrace to the game. You are a disgrace to your school. Who do you play for?'

'I play for Assumption College, Kilmore. We were playing against Scotch College.'

'Oh,' said the priest, rubbing his sleeve, 'boys will be boys.'

★ It was said about a certain footballer's biography: 'This is not a book to be tossed aside lightly, it should be thrown with great force into the smallest room in the house and used page by page.'

★ Then there was the intellectual player who, when filling in his application form, wrote under:

Age: Nuclear

Sex: Frequently

Previous clubs: Casino, Caulfield Racing and the RACV.

★ The coach and the club president are celebrating a Grand Final win.

The coach says as he lowers his glass, 'Tell me—would you have liked me as much if we had lost?'

'Of course I would,' the president replied. 'But I would have missed you.'

★ The decisions had not really gone their way, and they were well and truly beaten. As they were walking off the field, the captain smiled sweetly and said to the umpire, 'Good game, too bad you didn't get to see it.'

★ I think he was the one who went to the club doctor and said he had a pain. He thought he needed a hernia transplant.

★ He wasn't the brightest player in the team. In fact, he thought Shirley Temple was a synagogue.

★ The chairman of the AFL tribunal: 'This is your fifth visit before the tribunal. I told you the last time, I didn't want to see you again.'

'I know,' replied the dual Brownlow medallist and Carlton champion Greg Williams . . . 'and I told that to the umpire, but he wouldn't listen to me!'

★ In the middle of the training oval, the coach addresses the players.

'Right, I have just one last move to teach you, Now all of you form a tight circle around me.'

The players duly gathered around him.

'Now I want you to run towards the dressing sheds.'

'But coach,' said one player, 'when will we need to move like this?'

'Well, the way you guys have been playing,' said the coach, 'I'll need it after every game.'

★ Then there was the player who failed his coach's certificate exam twelve times.

He could run, kick, tackle and jump but he couldn't pass.

★ The difference between a great player and a brilliant player is this: a great player should only believe half of what he reads about himself.

A brilliant player knows which half!

★ Probably as bad as 'You have lovely eyes. I could live in them.'

And she countered, 'You'd be at home—there's a sty in one of them.'

★ The superstar player who felt that his prowess on the football field had given him a way to success with the ladies was chatting up what he hoped would be his latest conquest.

'How about, after the game, back to my place a few quiet drinks and some soft music?' he whispered in what he thought was his most seductive voice.

And she said, 'I'm afraid my awareness of your proclivities in the esoteric aspects of sexual behaviour precludes such an erotic confrontation.'

'I don't get it,' he said.

'Exactly,' she smiled.

★ Some said he had a chip on his shoulder. He didn't have a chip. He had a whole timber yard!!

★ The saddest thing about going away on an end-of-season trip is . . . when you are so old, you can't take 'yes' for an answer!

★ His opening line left a little to be desired: 'I'd love to see you in a two-piece outfit—a pair of slippers.'

★ Here's a moral question: the day before the Grand Final Gary Ablett, the mercurial Geelong full forward goes to church to pray for victory, and there, lying on the seat beside him was the opposition team's match plan.

Now the question is this: 'Was this a temptation by the devil or the answer to his prayers?'

★ First supporter says: 'Did you know that the army has developed a powerful air gas that when used could produce inertia and put people to sleep for days?'

The second supporter says, 'Does it really work?'

The first guy said, 'Well they never found out, they tested it on the Adelaide Crows' bus to Melbourne and nobody could tell the difference.'

★ Manager of pub team to the players: 'I vote we train on Thursdays.'

A voice from the back: 'What, every Thursday?'

★ I think the real problem is that they start to play Little League too young. Last year the best and fairest went to a five-year-old.

And that was for going twelve consecutive games without wetting his pants.

★ He doesn't have the highest IQ in the team, which possibly explains why when the coach said 'Can you pass a football?' he replied, 'Yes sir, if I swallow it I can pass it.'

★ Definition of football: it's a game in which 36 big, strong, young men run around for 100 minutes while 50,000 people—people who really need the exercise—stand and watch them.

★ 'Umpire, you stink!'

'OK,' said the umpire as he pulled the player back a further 50 metres. 'Tell me—how do I smell from here?'

★ 'Don't you know it's a sin to play football on the Sabbath?'

'Well, the way we've been playing it certainly is,' answered the Demon supporter.

★ You can always tell the people who say 'Money can't buy a good football team.'

They are usually the ones with very little experience of either.

In owning a football club you get the special gift that permits a man to put two and two together and come up with any answer he likes.

★ They wanted me to play for them badly, which I did.

★ I hate favouritism in football teams and players who are not picked on their merits.

I just happen to like mowing the coach's lawn and washing his car.

★ 'Nunky' Ayers was known as Mr Football in Tasmania. On the invitation of team coach Noel Ruddock, he coached the Friends' School's first XVIII to a grand final victory against St Virgil's in 1966—only the third time in eighty-eight years that our school had won a football premiership, and a result to cherish.

Nunk delivered the half-time speech—a beauty.

'I can see 'em in there now, with their rosary beads,

crossing themselves and praying to the big fella upstairs to help them. But believe me, when they run out on the ground, hit 'em with everything you've got, and I promise you they'll bleed and hurt just like the rest of us!' he yelled and chopped the air with a flat hand, laying down the law. 'Now follow me!'

Nunk hunched his shoulders and ran like a wounded bull at the closed dressing-room door— BOOM, CRASH, CLUNK! The door was flattened. The human battering ram charged through. As captain I was first to follow.

He turned and thumped me in the chest. 'You make your ol' man proud of you, son!'

What had happened was that Nunky had gee'd up Val Evans, the curator, to remove the pins from the door hinges ten minutes earlier. Nunk hit the door from about seven metres in a wonderful show of strength—hip and shoulder. We never looked like losing. This was the Nunky Ayers special, perfected over many years, but it didn't always go the way of the coach. The occasion was a combined Huon Football Association team against the

Kingborough Country Football Association at Sandfly. This was the beginning of the running-through-the-hinged-door half-time theatre—many football identities have claimed it for their own, but Nunk was the first.

Big Max had wagered ten pounds (twenty dollars) on the Huon side. They were six goals behind at half-time, his money was not looking good.

Nunky alerted the caretaker to undo the door hinges to the adjoining door. It would require a screwdriver to remove the hinges from the door jamb.

'I want to see the blood rolling out of your eyes and ears, and attack those bastards with hip and shoulder as if running through a doorway!' The coach stormed the door, intending to show the way it was done—but unfortunately the caretaker either forgot to, or couldn't, find the screwdriver.

Nunk hit the door as though he was auditioning for a Hollywood movie. The door failed to budge, and Nunk ended up on his rump with an injured shoulder, embarrassed and the focus of everyone's laughter.

Climbing to his feet, he was ropable—like a gorilla gone mad. Big Max reckoned what followed would make the Ron Barassis, David Parkins and Alan Killigrews appear bland by comparison.

★ A great difference between school and football is that at school you were told to stand up for Jesus' sake and at football you are told to sit down for God's sake.

★ Up before the AFL Tribunal. The chairman says, 'This is your last season and we are looking for a reason not to suspend you. Can you verify, for instance, that you were under instruction to thump the back of your opponent's head?'

'Yes sir, the coach told me to do that, but I've got

to be honest—kicking him in the testicles was my own idea.'

★ People complain that a science professor only receives quarter of the wage of a football coach. But then I've never heard 90,000 students cheer the principle of Archimedes.

★ When I was a kid I played football with my sister —but it was useless, I mean—I couldn't bounce her.

★ They were sitting on the pavement, these two members of the twilight zone, and the first said, 'Do you know if you rub two one dollar coins together, you'll hear a noise like a football crowd?'

So the second bloke gets the two one dollar coins rubs them together and says, 'I can hear nothing.'

The first fella says, 'Must be half-time!'

★ The club was so exclusive, they would not even let the members in.

★ The secretary said to the club manager: 'We have videos of games played ten to twenty years ago and they are taking up a lot of space. Should I get rid of them?'

'Yes,' the manager replied. 'But before you do, make copies.'

★ We lost so many games that not only were we thrown out of the League but they had us registered as a charity.

★ I met Jack Dyer for the first time when I joined Channel Seven to be their cricket expert on the 'World of Sport' panel—what an education! Captain Blood was unforgettable.

His own description of himself was, 'I'm a legion. A champion team will always beat a team of champions, unless the team of champions is very very good!'

He is said to have often sat in his old Holden, parked outside the studios in Dorcas Street, reading the 'Births, Deaths and Marriages' section of the *Sun* newspaper, fascinated.

'How come everyone keeps dying in alphabetical order?' he'd ask Lou Richards.

One day, before 'World of Sport' went to air for the last time, he said to Louie, 'Geez, what's up with woodchopper Jack O'Toole? He never hangs around after the show any more. Have I said something wrong about him?'

Lou replied, 'Course he ain't hanging around no more. He died two years ago and you went to his funeral! That's only his voice they use, to start the wood-chopping, you dummy!'

The other one of his I like is: 'He was so slow I thought his stops had grown into the ground!' Or, 'That bloke's got no brains—he ought to go and see a nuclear physiotherapist!' And when told of the death of a former Carlton great during the program, he replied that it was 'a bit of bad luck for Bob'. Whether they are all true or not doesn't really matter. We love you, Jack, even if you did reckon I 'wouldn't get a kick in Tom Sherrin's football factory'.

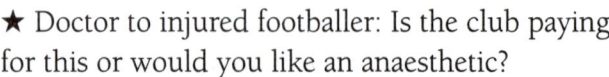

★ Doctor to injured footballer: Is the club paying for this or would you like an anaesthetic?

★ Newly retired footballers who go to the media, are like the Indians in a John Wayne movie.

They look good but you know they are not going to last.

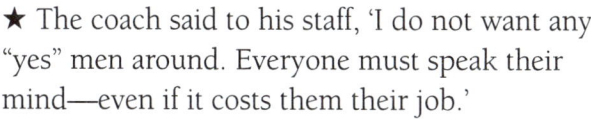

★ The coach said to his staff, 'I do not want any "yes" men around. Everyone must speak their mind—even if it costs them their job.'

★ Despite the fact that the character Crackers Keenan portrays on TV is some what gormless, his career would suggest an expert knowledge of the game.

Who can forget his Grand Final call of the Carlton–Essendon game, particularly since it was North Melbourne versus the Sydney Swans?

★ I'll tell you how good our club chairman is—he watches *Sesame Street* and doesn't understand it.

★ Robert Smith, the boss of North Melbourne Social Club who played over 100 games for North Melbourne denies he ever had a weight problem.

He says he's a light eater—which is true—as soon as it's light he eats.

He also says he just has a lot of fat that doesn't fit.

★ Drew Morphett describing Max Walker's radio commentary début:

At the end of the game Drew was asked how the 'big fella' had performed.

'This bloke's unreal,' Drew replied. 'He can talk underwater with a mouth full of marbles!'

★ Of course the best diet in the world is to eat all you want of everything you don't like.

Or, better still, only eat when Brisbane Broncos and Collingwood tie for first place in a popularity contest.

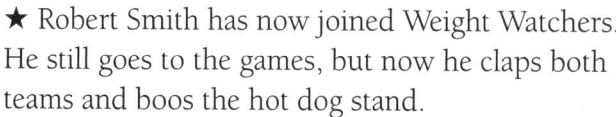

★ Robert Smith has now joined Weight Watchers. He still goes to the games, but now he claps both teams and boos the hot dog stand.

★ Kevin Sheedy, one of the game's great minds is trying to console his players at Essendon this season.

'We've still got a shot at the flag, boys,' said Sheeds, 'all we've gotta do is win 10 of our next 5 games!'

★ When Ted Whitten died he went straight to heaven. On his arrival he greeted St Peter with the bone-crushing signature handshake and another saint with the squirrel grip. God certainly knew Teddy had arrived . . . and on meeting God said that although Ted had been feisty and colourful on earth, he could have one wish.

'That's easy!' said Ted. 'I want a team made up of the greatest players of all time: Norm Smith, who could coach, Laurie Nash, Peter Crimmins, Fred Fanning, Reg Hickey, Gordon Coventry . . . what a bunch to select from!'

God granted Ted his wish and after the team of greats assembled, he got a call from the Devil inviting him for a game.

'You're crazy!' shouted Ted. 'We've got all the good players.'

'Sure,' said Satan, 'but we've got the umpires!'

Golf

★Give me my golf clubs
the fresh air and a
beautiful girl for a
partner—and you can
keep my golf clubs and
the fresh air.

—Jack Benny

★ A wise man once said, 'Golf is an adult's way of playing marbles.'

★ Golfers are nothing if not inconsistent. You hit a bad shot, you blame God or the wind.

You score a hole in one, and you take all the credit for yourself.

★ 'As I lie here dying I have one last request. Even though I feel that I was handicapped out of winning the club championship I would like you and the other golf club directors to stand for a minute's silence at my grave.'

'Certainly George, that is the least we can do for you. Where are you being buried?'

'Hopefully at sea!'

★ The old leather-faced golfer paced anxiously up and down outside the emergency room of the hospital near the golf course. Inside the doctors were operating to remove a golf ball accidentally driven up a player's 'clacker'.

The sister-in-charge noticed the anxious old golfer and went to reassure him.

'It won't be long now sir,' she said. 'You're a relative?'

'No, no, miss. That's my bloody ball and I want it back no matter what the condition!'

★ Then there were the Siamese twins who said to the golf pro, 'I wonder if we could have a tee for two.'

★ The disenchanted player took to the whiskey in the clubhouse. The drunk had been looking for a fight all day since losing his game. Finally he threw a real 'haymaker' at the player parked on the nearest bar stool. The target ducked and the drunk swung himself completely off his stool and on to the floor!

By the time he'd composed his limp body from the fallen bar stools and dusted himself off, his opponent had bolted.

'What did you make of that, barman?' he complained. 'Not much of a fighter, was he?'

Not much of a driver either, sir. He's just driven the four-wheel drive over your clubs,' the barman said, gesturing to the carpark.

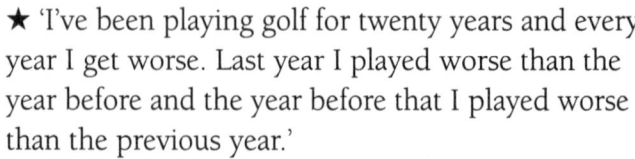

★ 'I've been playing golf for twenty years and every year I get worse. Last year I played worse than the year before and the year before that I played worse than the previous year.'

'That's sad,' said his mate, 'but how are you playing now?'

He said through clenched teeth, 'I am already playing next year's game.'

★ Nothing counts in a golf game like your opponent.

★ The eighty-year-old golfer's wife gives birth to a seven-month-old baby.

He was so excited. 'Imagine that—two under par and me with a whippy shaft.'

★ 'Honestly, I took nine hours to play my round,' an anxious husband was explaining to his furious wife.

'What! For eighteen holes?' his wife asked in obvious disbelief.

'Well fourteen, actually. Reggie died of a heart attack on the fourth and it's very slow progress when you have to hit the ball, drag a body, hit the ball, drag a body, and so on!!!

★ Greg Norman woke up one morning and said, 'I feel like a million dollars.'

And his wife says, 'Why are you so depressed?'

★ The caddie says, 'It's a difficult hole. I've played here before—use a three wood.'

'No, I think I'll use a five iron.'

They have a terrible row, and eventually he uses a five iron and he has a hole in one.

'Well, what do you think of that?' he asks the caddie.

'Well,' said the disgruntled caddie, 'I still think that you'd have done better with a three wood.'

★ Let me tell you how bad a golfer he is. In his bag he carries flares, a compass and emergency rations.

★ Tries to putt in from seventy metres out and the spectator said, 'Who does he think he is—God?'

The second spectator said, 'It is God. He thinks he is Greg Norman.'

★ I was under par after only four holes. Lovely man, Par!

★ 'That can't be my ball, caddie. It Looks far too old.'
  'It's a long time since we started, sir.'

★ Roger said, 'I got a new set of clubs for my wife!'
  The second player comments, 'That's a good bargain.'

★ The caddie said, 'It's a pity you didn't take up golf sooner.'
  The golfer: 'What do you mean? I'd be better now.'

The caddie: ' No, you would have given it up a long time ago.'

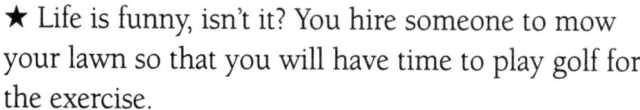

★ Life is funny, isn't it? You hire someone to mow your lawn so that you will have time to play golf for the exercise.

★ There were no flowers on the coffin, just a set of golf clubs.

One mourner said, 'He must have been a keen golfer—they are burying his clubs with him.'

'Not really,' said the second mourner, 'it's his wife's funeral and he is playing a round afterwards.'

★ The wife is in full flight. 'If you ever spent a Sunday with me instead of playing golf I swear I would drop dead.'

He said, 'Listen dear, There's no point in trying to bribe me.'

★ 'What's your handicap?'

'My wife, she won't let me play.'

★ A newcomer was to learn the great game at Melbourne's Albert Park Public Golf Course.

'And how does one play this game?' he asked his hired coach.

The coach explained about teeing off, the course, and his clubs—the irons and woods and so on, but he finished by saying:

'Basically Richard, all you have to do is hit the ball in the direction of that flag over there.'

'Right ho,' and the novice teed off. It was a magnificent drive that took the flight of his ball right down the centre of the fairway. And, unbelievably, it landed on the green only to roll a few centimetres from the hole.

'What do I do now?' asked the novice.

'Just hit the ball into the hole sir,' said the coach in some excitement. 'That's the whole idea of the game!'

'Why didn't you tell me that before I hit off?'

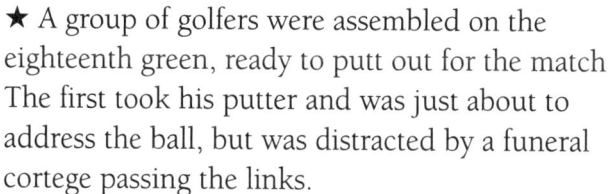

★ A group of golfers were assembled on the eighteenth green, ready to putt out for the match. The first took his putter and was just about to address the ball, but was distracted by a funeral cortege passing the links.

As he watched it crawl by, he took his hat off, held it to his chest, and burst into tears.

'You seem awfully upset', one of his party said, 'after all, it's just a funeral'.

'Upset?' he replied, 'Why wouldn't I be? She gave me twenty-five good years.'

★ 'How long have you been playing golf for?'

'Just two weeks. Mind you, it took me four years to learn.'

★ 'Did you win at golf today, Dad?' asked the five-year-old.

'Well son, I hit the ball more times than anybody else out there!'

★ Business tycoon Robert had just come in from an extended afternoon on the golf course. His wife Pam kissed him and kissed their son who lobbed in a few seconds later.

'Where's he been?' the husband asked.

'He's been caddying for you all afternoon,' the man's wife replied.

'No wonder that kid looked so familiar!'

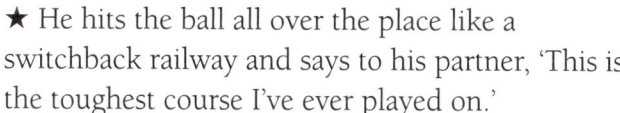

★ He hits the ball all over the place like a switchback railway and says to his partner, 'This is the toughest course I've ever played on.'

His partner says, 'How would you know? You haven't played on it yet.'

★ Is that my friend in the sand trap? Or did that bastard get on the green?

★ The ultimate golf lie: 'They may have looked like extra strokes to you, but I was actually killing a snake.'

★ Ken joined a foursome; and as he'd had a very successful day he was invited back the next day. 8 a.m. tee off time.

'Look, I'd sure like to play,' said Ken, 'but I could be two minutes late!'

Next morning he showed up right on the dot, played another fine round, but this time he played every stroke left-handed.

Again, he was invited to join the threesome at 8 a.m. the following morning.

'Sure, I'll be here,' said Ken, 'but remember I could be late, but it will only be a couple of minutes!'

'We'll wait,' one of the golfers assured him. 'But by the way, could you explain something that's been mystifying us all. Yesterday you played *right-handed* and today you played *left-handed*. Obviously you're proficient at both so how do you decide which way to play?'

'Ah,' Ken answered, 'when I wake up in the morning, if my wife's lying on her right side, I play *right-handed* and if she's lying on her left side, I play *left-handed*. Simple as that.'

'But what if she's lying on her back?'

'Well, that's when I'm two minutes late!' he grinned.

★ She said to her husband 'My golf is improving. Yesterday I hit a ball in one.'

★ I once played against Greg Norman. There was just one point in it—he was 68 and I was 168.

★ I actually believe that being buried with your golf clubs is a stupid idea.

Imagine—if St Peter sees you arrive with a set of clubs you'd have to convince him that you've never ever told a lie. Tough assignment.

★ I once played golf with a very much overweight Marlon Brando.

When he teed off on the front nine, he cast a shadow over the back nine.

★ Marlon Brando is the only golfer who carries his own foursome.

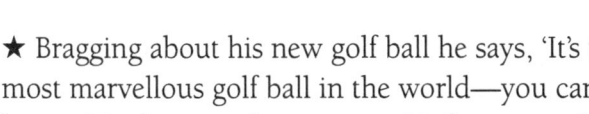

★ Bragging about his new golf ball he says, 'It's the most marvellous golf ball in the world—you cannot lose it. You hit it in the water and it floats, you hit it in the rough and it beeps, so that you can hear it. You cannot lose it.'

'Where did you get it?'

'I found it.'

Unfortunately the first time he hit it it caught fire.

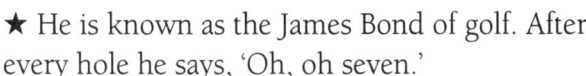

★ He is known as the James Bond of golf. After every hole he says, 'Oh, oh seven.'

★ Location: Royal Canberra Golf Club. Former Prime Minister Bob Hawke on the first tee.

'Sir, I understand you must probably be a new member here, but even you should know that you cannot take your first shot three metres ahead of the marker.'

The PM ignored the comment and continued to address the ball.

'Listen, I am chairman of the greens. I must remind you to go back behind the white markers. Otherwise I'll have to report you to the board.'

Eventually Bob looked up and replied, 'Let me tell you three things, mate. In the first place, you are annoying the shitter out of me.

'In the second place, I have been a member of this club for nearly twelve months now.

'In the third place, this is my second bloody shot. Now shut up and let me continue the game.'

★ He hit his drive into the rough where he hit a quail.

As he said later, it was the first time 'he had hit a partridge on a par three'.

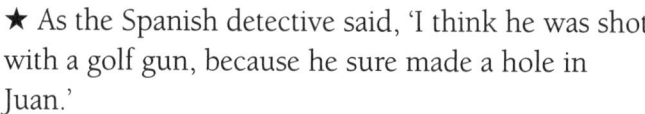

★ As the Spanish detective said, 'I think he was shot with a golf gun, because he sure made a hole in Juan.'

★ She had read a lot about golf and wanting to brag about her knowledge on her first day on the course, she asked the club pro, 'Excuse me, which club do I use for a hole in one?'

★ He sliced three successive balls into the river, and then had to ask his partner to loan him a ball, and then another ball, and then a third ball.

Eventually, his partner said, 'Hold on James, golf balls cost money. I'm not going to give you any more just so you can slice them into the river.'

James threw his bags and clubs down in disgust and said, 'I'm off. I don't know why you are still a member of this club if you can't afford to play the game.'

★ At the National seaside course in Victoria a novice managed a mighty drive off the second tee. It hit, and bounced off in rapid succession, a rock outcrop, a fisherman, a tree trunk, the handle of a golf buggy, a birdwatcher, a player on the second tee and finally it dropped onto the green about fifteen centimetres from the pin.

'Well,' the youngster exclaimed, 'if only I'd hit the ball a bit bloody harder!'

★ She had seen better days, this faded beauty, and was back in the club house after her first round of golf.

'Oh,' she said, 'it was so exciting. I was down after taking three shots on the seventh.'

Her friends said that that was fantastic.

'Yes', she said. 'Unfortunately, then the green keeper came and ordered us off.

★ 'You are driving me mad!' exclaimed the wife.

'Hardly dear, at the most it would be just a short putt.'

★ 'If I died, would you remarry?' asked his wife Wendy.

'Probably would,' came the muffled reply.

'And would you let her be your golfing partner?'

'Yes, sure.'

'But surely you wouldn't give her my clubs? Would you?'

'Nah . . . she's left-handed.'

★ A yell from the woods: 'Hey caddie! Never mind the ball. Come and find me!'

★ The game had taken hours—he had continually rejected the caddie's advice.

Eventually, in total frustration, he shouted at the caddie, 'Shut up! I was playing this game before you were born.'

'Yes,' said the caddie, 'but I'm trying to get you to finish it before I die.'

★ 'Look at that idiot using the wood for his second shot. The last fellow who did that broke that . . . DUCK!'

★ Do you know Greg Norman once went round in ten under par?

Can you believe that? Sixty-two lucky shots in succession.

★ 'Golf is the most stupid game in the world.'

'I agree with you and I am glad I don't have to play it until tomorrow.'

★ 'How's your golf?'

'Well, let me tell you I am playing so badly that I am just going to buy a bucket of balls so that I can practise my drop.'

★ He had just been presented with the club's 'Best Golfer of the Year' award. In his acceptance speech he said, 'This is mainly due to my wife, because at the start of the year she and I agreed that if we ever had an argument the one who was wrong would have to leave the house and do his own thing for a couple of hours. If I lost I would go and practise putting, and if my wife lost she would go work in the garden for a couple of hours.

'And that is why, gentlemen, I am now putting better than ever and my garden is looking worse than ever.'

★ I will admit that I am not the best golfer in the world. In fact, I once played nine holes and lost eleven clubs.

★ Last year when playing golf with the Archbishop of Canterbury, and despite his obvious respect for the company, when he missed a three-foot putt he screamed out at the top of his voice, 'Bugger it—I missed it!'

Needless to say the Archbishop was not amused and he said so.

Two holes later the same thing happened, and the same reaction, 'Oh bugger, I missed.'

The Archbishop said, 'God does not like that sort of language or indeed that lack of self-control. Any more swearing and I hazard a guess that God will take his revenge.'

Well, eventually Tom takes control and they are all square going into the last hole. Tom needs a three-foot putt to win. He misses. He begins a flow of blasphemy that would do credit to Satan's lip.

Suddenly, there is a clap of thunder and a flash of lightning, and the Archbishop drops dead.

The voice from the heavens says, 'Oh bugger, I missed.'

★ 'My wife says that if I don't give up golf she'll leave me.'

'Say, that's a bit rough, mate.'

'Yeah, I'm really going to miss her.'

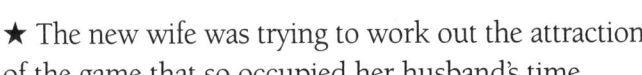

★ The new wife was trying to work out the attraction of the game that so occupied her husband's time.

'What is a handicapped golfer?' she asked.

'One who plays with his boss,' came the rapid reply.

★ The doctor says to the out-of-form golfer, 'I am afraid that I have some good news and some bad news for you. The bad news is that there is something peculiar happening in your body. And you are due for a change of sex.'

'Oh my goodness', said the golfer. 'What's the good news?'

'Ah', said the doctor. 'The good news is that you can now play off the ladies' tee.'

★ The Reverend Fred Nile is playing golf and he hits a terrible shot. The ball hits a tree, bounces on to a rock, does a right angle and then is adorned by some radar beam, rolls over the apron across the green, hits the pin and drops into the hole—a hole in one.

The astounded Reverend looks up to heaven and says 'Lord, if you don't mind I'd rather do it myself.'

★ They were golfing mates and he died. But months later he came back in a vision, 'Hi mate, What's heaven like?'

'Well, it's good and bad. The good news is that its golf course is absolutely magnificent and the bad news is that next week you're playing on it.'

★ True golfers—they protect their handicaps more than their wife's.

★ 'Golf is a funny game.'

How many times have we heard that? The sad thing of course is that it's not meant to be funny.

★ Did you hear about the player who spent so much time in the bunker he got mail addressed to Hitler?

★ The chairman was annoyed at the golf club's new steward.

'Do you know who I am?' he demanded.

'No, sir,' was the reply 'but I'll make some enquiries and then I'll come back and tell you.'

★ 'It was the worst day I've ever had at golf—I hit a spectator in the head with the golf ball.'

'Come on, a lot of players have done that.'

'I know, but I was putting at the time.'

★ Talk about fantastic golf teachers. He was the best and one day this woman came up to him and said that she had developed a terrific slice.

Day and night he worked with her for five months. Now she's the biggest hooker in town.

★ The ultimate cheat in golf—he once shot a hole in one and on the score card he wrote zero.

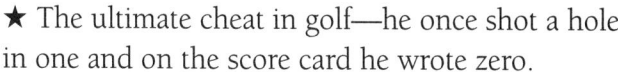

★ Life is so unfair. A good golfer has to break 80, whereas a sweet young thing only has to bust 36.

★ I once played golf with a country bank manager. Every time I yelled fore, he yelled closure.

★ Judge: 'Do you understand the nature of an oath?'
  Boy: 'I'm your caddie, remember?'

★ She joined the public golf course and became a wonderful golfer.

So she joined another golf course and in no time at all she became an intercourse champion.

★ The Bishop is trying subtly to get his partner to temper his language.

'I have observed in life', he said, 'that the best golfers are not addicted to bad language.'

His partner, who was hitting a ball out of a sand trap, said as the ball rolled to a stop between his anchored feet, 'Hell, what the fucking hell have they got to swear about?'

★ Knock–knock.

Who's there?

Adolf.

Adolf who?

Adolf ball hit me in the mouth and that's why I talk funny!

★ 'You were putting so well, how come you've improved so much?'

'Well,' said Bruce, 'these glasses I'm wearing are bifocals so when I look through the edges of the two lenses I see two balls—one big, one small, and two holes—one small, one big, and from then on it's easy. I just knock the small ball into the big hole.'

★ The golf pro: 'Now, I just want you to practise your swing without hitting the ball.'

Learner: 'That is exactly the trouble I am trying to overcome.'

★ An exclusive golf club is a place where you can meet the kind of people you would have black-balled if you had gotten in first.

★ 'If you spend so much time at golf you won't have anything laid aside for a rainy day.'

'Oh, won't I just! You should see my desk. It's just groaning with the work that I've set aside for a rainy day.'

★ 'My doctor says I can't play golf.'

   'Oh, I didn't know he had seen you play.'

★ 'I think,' said Father Finn, 'I'll use a three iron. I'll just take a full swing and pray.'

   He did and the ball fell into the sand trap.

   Priest: 'I guess the good God didn't hear me.'

   'Oh I don't know,' said the club pro, 'in our church when we pray we keep our heads down.'

★ What's so good about Tiger Woods?

   If I had his talent and dedication I could play just as well.

★ My golf pro only studied my game for a mere three minutes and gave me the best piece of advice for improving my game.

Head down, eye on the ball, and cheat.

★ He was new to golf. First game, in fact. He was a generous man and after the 18 holes he said to the club pro, 'What should I give my caddie?'

And the club pro said, 'How about your clubs?'

★ Blind man meets Greg Norman and says, 'I've always wanted to play you at golf.'

Norman says 'I'd be delighted, but let's have a little condition. Whoever wins buys the other a beer.'

'Well,' says the blind man, 'I was thinking $500 a hole.'

'$500 a hole?' said Norman, 'that's a lot of money, but if that's the way you want it so be it. When do you want to play?'

And the blind man said, 'At midnight!'

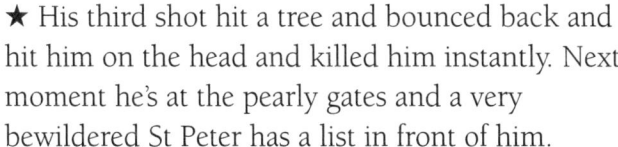

★ His third shot hit a tree and bounced back and hit him on the head and killed him instantly. Next moment he's at the pearly gates and a very bewildered St Peter has a list in front of him.

'Well,' said St Peter, 'at last I've found your name, but it says here you're not due for another twenty years. How did you get here?'

'In three,' the golfer replied.

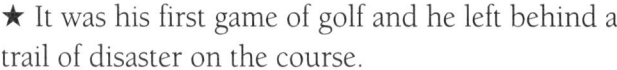

★ It was his first game of golf and he left behind a trail of disaster on the course.

He's back at the club house and because it was his first round he's celebrating, when a discreet voice says, 'Excuse me sir, but I'm the chairman of the greens committee.'

And the new golfer looks up from his plate and says, 'Just the bloke I want to see. These brussels sprouts are bloody terrible.'

★ Greg Norman is one of the highest paid sportsmen in the world. He's making so much money he has a drive-in wallet.

★ There's been a punch-up in the club house and the first golfer called before the committee gives an interpretation of the fight. And the chairman says, 'Yes, you are so right.' The first golfer leaves the room.

The second golfer comes in, and gives an entirely different interpretation.

And the chairman says, 'Thank you, you are so right.'

By this time his assistant is totally confused and says to the chairman, 'How can you tell both of them they are right? They both can't be right.'

The Chairman says, 'You are so right.'

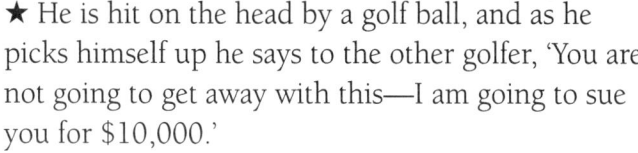

★ He is hit on the head by a golf ball, and as he picks himself up he says to the other golfer, 'You are not going to get away with this—I am going to sue you for $10,000.'

And the second golfer said, 'Hold on, I said four.'

And the first golfer said, 'I'll take it.'

★ Saw a sign in the pro shop: 'Ring for Service'. So he did and a tennis ball hit him in the face.

★ He hit a great shot which unfortunately landed over the trees, well and truly in the sticks. And his partner, who had his back turned to him, said, 'Hey, that sounded mighty good.'

'You're not wrong,' he replied. 'But unfortunately I'm playing golf and not giving a concert!'

★ A couple of golfers were telling tall stories about their powers at golf.

'Well,' said the first, 'I once mishit a ball and it must have gone 150 yards, broke a window, hit an oil lamp knocked it over and the place caught fire.'

'What did you do?'

He said, 'Well, I very carefully teed another ball, steadied myself, used my driver, hit the ball as hard as I knew how. The ball zinged through the air, onto the main road and hit the fire alarm back at the club house. And within two minutes the fire brigade were on the scene and put out the fire.'

★ At times the hardest thing about the game of golf is being allowed out of the house to play it.

★ 'Yes, he plays a fair game of golf.'
  'You're right, but only when you watch him.'

★ Life is a game of golf—you're out of one hole and then you are into another.

★ He took a wild swing at the golf ball and missed by the proverbial mile. But quick as a flash he said to his partner, 'Do you know that this course is at least four inches lower than the one I normally play on?'

★ Q: What do have when you have a golf ball in your left hand and a golf ball in your right hand?

   A: A very big golf.

★ It was a good annual dinner. The president gave a short speech because of his throat.

After last year's speech, several members threatened to cut it.

★ Ad in newspaper:
'Must sell golf clubs, Or get a divorce.'

★ 'I'd move heaven and earth to get my handicap down to single figures.'

'Well, try heaven', said his partner, 'you've already moved enough earth.'

★ My golf is improving. Today I hit a ball in one.

★ There is a strong theory that golf balls will last longer if kept in a refrigerator.

There is another theory that they will last even longer if they are left in the refrigerator.

★ Then there was the big game hunter who took up golf.

His biggest disappointment was when he played a good shot, he couldn't get it stuffed.

★ Left his golf clubs beside his car with a note saying: 'These prize clubs belong to a fitness fanatic who is an ex-marine, a heavyweight boxer and also an expert in karate and kung fu and I will be back in five minutes.'

When he came back the clubs were gone and in their place was a little note saying: 'Your clubs have been taken by a 400 m Olympic champion, and I won't be back at all.'

★ What's your handicap?

Three: I can't drive, I can't putt and I don't like the game.

★ Golf fanatic is never at home. First time he turned up late for a game.

'Sorry I'm late—my wife broke my driver.'

'You can borrow mine.'

'I know, but that won't stop my head from throbbing.'

★ Someone once said of golfer Gary Player: 'I've seen him drive—he hit the ball further than I go on holidays.'

★ The day he got a hole in one, I saw the state he was in when he got home. He roared into his driveway, clipped the tree, tore up the garden, ran over his kid's bicycle and smashed into the garage door. Mind you, it could have been worse.

Can you imagine the damage he would have done if he had been driving a car?

★ A golf pro was approached by two ladies.

'Do you wish to learn to play golf, Ma'am?' he asked one.

'Oh no', she said, 'it is my friend who wants to learn, I learnt yesterday.'

★ 'Don't think', she said to her husband, 'you are going to sneak off and play golf and leave me here to do all the work.'

The husband protested. 'Golf is the furthest thing from my mind, and would you please pass the putter?'

★ It was their second day playing. She closed her eyes, took an almighty swing, hooked to the right, the club ricocheted off two trees, took a fantastic bounce, killed a pigeon in mid-flight hit another golfer on the head and rolled into the cup for a hole in one.

The second lady said very coldly, 'Judith, you are a sneak. You've been practising.'

★ A male foursome was being held up by two slow lady golfers, one of whom was searching in the rough.

'Why don't you help your friend look for her ball and let us get on with our game?'

'Oh, she's not looking for her ball,' said the woman. 'She's looking for her club.'

★ Do not trust him: he's a con man and, worse than that, he cheats at golf.

'Oh, do you know him personally?'

'Know him? I taught him everything he knows.'

★ Had a good day at golf today—I found more balls than I lost.

★ You may not know this, but the greatest cause of heart attacks for male golfers over 60 is female golfers under 30.

★ This man is so well adjusted he can play golf as though it was just another game.

★ Life is sad. By the time you can afford to lose a golf ball you can't hit it that far.

★ Before I became a full-time golfer I was a door-to-door salesman selling wall-to-wall carpeting and back-to-back tape on a day-to-day basis with 50—50 commission in Wagga Wagga.

'How was business?'

'So-so.'

★ One of the advantages of ten-pin bowling over golf is that you very seldom lose a bowling ball.

★ They called it golf because all the other four-letter words were taken.

★ I partnered Greg Norman in the club foursomes.

At least I think it was Greg Norman—because when he we were beaten my partner said, 'If you're a golfer, I'm Greg Norman.'

But he must have really liked me, because at the end of the day he said, I was on his hit list.

★ The golf pro rushed his pregnant wife to hospital. Unfortunately they didn't quite make it, and she gave birth on the lawn outside the hospital.

The hospital, in its infinite wisdom, not only charged him for delivery but also an extra $20 for green fees.

★ A well-known solicitor's wife asked him why he never would let her play golf with him.

'Rebecca,' he replied, 'there are three things a man must do alone: testify, die and putt.'

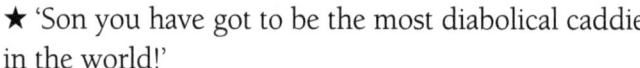

★ A golfing man of the cloth had been comprehensively beaten by one of his flock. He returned to the clubhouse, disappointed and a little depressed.

'Cheer up,' said his opponent. 'Remember, you win at the finish. You'll probably be burying me some day.'

'Yes, but even then,' said the priest, 'it will still be your hole.'

★ 'Son you have got to be the most diabolical caddie in the world!'

'Absolutely impossible, sir. That would be just too much of a coincidence.'

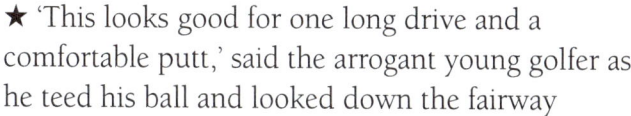

★ It was a golfing holiday in Ireland and like all good golfing holidays the nineteenth hole was getting a workout. The debate was as to which whiskey was the stronger: Scotch or Irish.

The visitor said, 'I'm certain it's Irish. A few nights ago the wife and I drank a bottle of it and the next morning we got up and went to six o'clock mass.'

'What's so unusual about that?'

'Well you see,' said the visitor, 'we're both Jewish.'

★ 'This looks good for one long drive and a comfortable putt,' said the arrogant young golfer as he teed his ball and looked down the fairway towards the green. He swung with all his might like a tree-felling contestant. His ball unfortunately landed only about a metre from his tee.

His caddie handed him a club and remarked: 'And now for one hell of a putt.'

★ 'I've heard a Croatian reckons he has invented a game which closely resembles golf.'

'Really, my husband's been playing that one for years.'

★ 'I gather you make more money in one year than the President Bill Clinton', a nosy stranger asked a leading touring professional.

'Yeah, well why not?' came the reply. 'I'm a much better player than he is.'

★ Said a patient whose doctor is always on the golf course: 'Nowadays, the only people making house calls are burglars.'

★ Next time you are lying on the operating table, remember that the guy who is about to perform the delicate surgery is the same guy who only yesterday missed a two-inch putt.

★ Tickets for the Australian Open are hard to get and the scalpers have a field day. One keen spectator and Greg Norman was offered a ticket for the final round for $150.

'That's crazy,' the enthusiast declared. 'Why, I could get a woman for that sort of money!'

'True sir, but with this ticket you get eighteen holes!'

★ Isn't it therapeutic to get out on the old golf course again and lie in the sun?

★ 'You think so much of your bloody golf game that you don't even remember when we were married.'

'Of course I do, darling. That was the incredible day I sunk that monster ten metre putt.'

★ The club secretary was apologetic. 'I'm sorry, sir, but we have no time open on the course today.'

'Now just a minute,' the member rejoined. 'What if I told you Mr Kerry Packer and partner wanted a game. Could you find a starting time for them?'

'Yes, of course I would.'

'Well, I happen to know that he's in England at the moment, so we'll take his time. OK?'

★ It was a superb addressing of the ball, a magnificent swing—but, somehow, a shocker of a slice resulted. The captain's ball collected a man at full force and down he went like a bag of wet cement.

The captain and his partner ran up to the unfortunate victim who lay spread-eagled on the fairway. He was quite unconscious and between his legs rested the tiny white ball.

'My goodness,' cried the captain with considerable concern. 'What should I do?'

'Probably ought not to move him,' said his partner, 'so he now becomes an immovable obstruction, and you can either play the ball as it lies or drop it two club-lengths away.'

★ 'I'm going to have to give up golf,' Kenny sadly advised the club secretary. 'I've become so nearsighted I keep losing balls and if I play with my glasses on they keep falling off.'

'Listen, don't give up mate,' the secretary replied. 'What about teaming up with old Roger Raymond?'

'But he's in his 80s and can barely make it around the course.'

'Yes, yes, he's old, but he's also farsighted and he'll be able to see exactly where you've hit your ball. It's one way to keep on playing.'

The next day Kenny and old Roger played their first round together. Ken teed off first and his aggressive swing sent the ball sailing down the fairway nearly 300 metres.

'Did you see it?' he asked Roger.

'Yes,' the old-timer answered.

'Where did it go?'

'I've forgotten!' came the honest reply.

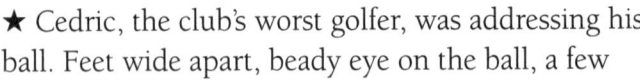

★ Cedric, the club's worst golfer, was addressing his ball. Feet wide apart, beady eye on the ball, a few nervous practice flutters with the driver, then an almighty great swing! He completely missed. The procedure was repeated and then, again! On the fourth swing however, he did manage to make contact with his ball and drove it five metres down the fairway. Looking up in sheer exasperation he saw a stranger who had stopped to watch him.

'Look here!' Cedric shouted angrily. 'Only fair dinkum golfers are allowed on this course!'

The stranger nodded, 'I know, mister,' he replied. 'But I won't say anything, if you won't either!'

★ 'You're late teeing off, William.'

'Yeah, well it being Sunday I had to toss a coin to see whether I should go to church or come to golf.'

'But why so late?'

'Well, I had to toss ten times, didn't I?'

★ 'Caddie, why do you keep looking at your watch, pal?'

'It ain't a watch, sir, it's a compass.'

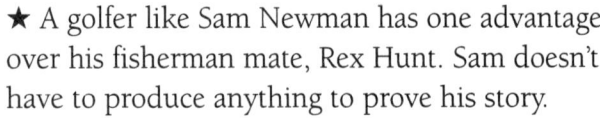

★ A golfer like Sam Newman has one advantage over his fisherman mate, Rex Hunt. Sam doesn't have to produce anything to prove his story.

★ Golfer: 'Notice any improvement today, Rupert?'

Caddie: 'Yes, luv. You've had your hair permed!'

★ 'I say, what happened to you, Fatty?' enquired the secretary of the Country Club.

The player whom he addressed was sitting staring straight ahead, a neat whisky in one hand and his bandaged head in the other.

'Extraordinary business really. Hooked my drive on the thirteenth. Ball landed in a cow-pat just off the fairway. Couldn't find the bloody thing.'

'How frustrating. But what happened? Did the cow charge at you?'

'No, no. I was standin' there wondering when an old dear playing behind me hit off. Hooked her ball too . . . same direction as mine. So I thought . . . find her ball and maybe I find mine.'

'Do go on, Fatty.'

'I was looking everywhere and one of those local cows walked past and swished up its tail . . . I couldn't believe my eyes, there was a golf ball wedged firmly in the grip of the large sphincter muscle. Too far away though to know if it was my ball or hers.'

'Yes?' nodding in agreement so far.

'Just then the lady climbed over the fence and

questioned me. 'Have you seen a red dot no. 4 golf ball?' Of course silly old me walked over to the cow, gently raised its tail and enquired, 'Look like yours?'

That's when she wrapped her 5 iron over my cranium!'

★ Jack and Jill were beginning a round of golf. Jill walked onto the tee, and her first drive presented her a hole in one. Jack stepped up to the tee and said, 'Now I'll have my practice swing . . . then we'll start the game, OK?'

Rugby League

★Sometimes we get so worked up over football, we almost wish it was a game.

—*E.C. McKenzie*

★ Two old rugby pros reminiscing:

'Things were much simpler when we played—our only tactical move was to get the ball and kick ahead.'

'Aye,' said the second prop, 'any head.'

★ Warren Ryan, one of the great modern Rugby League coaches, did it his way, which, to put it mildly, can cause conflict with club directors. We did some TV shows together and someone asked him what it was like working with a comedian.

Warren replied, 'I'm used to it. I worked with nine of them at ••••'.

★ 'How did you know you were dropped from the side?'

'Well, the manager told me visitors were no longer welcome in the dressing room.' Can't beat bad luck!

★ He was a fanatical fan who cheered every move his team made. He cheered and shouted and screamed. His voice started to go. He turned to the man beside him: 'I think I've lost my voice.'

'Don't worry,' he replied. 'You'll find it in my right ear.' I can relate to that!

★ If two illegal tackles cannot get you to score, try three!

★ Kevin Ryan was one of the toughest players ever to play for St George. When he tackled you, after you woke up . . . all you wanted to know was the number plate of the car.

★ Kevin Ryan was equally tough as a coach. At training one night, one player screamed in agony, 'I've just broken my leg.'

The coach's reply was, 'Well, don't just lie there, do some press-ups.'

★ When Kevin Ryan tackles you, people look at you after the game and say, 'Can I have a word in your eye?'

★ Tough: beside him Arnie Schwarzenegger is a cartoon.

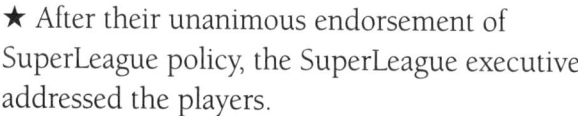

★ After their unanimous endorsement of SuperLeague policy, the SuperLeague executive addressed the players.

'Right, lads. Now that you have voted freely and without coercion you may lower your arms and come away from the wall.'

★ 'Listen coach,' said the new player, 'I know you think I'm a bit of a playboy, but let me assure you I am a man of regular habit.'

'Is that so,' said the coach. 'How come I heard you were in a bar at 4 a.m. with a girl young enough to be your daughter?'

'Well, like I said, coach, that's one of my regular habits.'

★ Our club just bought a new conference table: 8 feet wide, 22 feet long, and sleeps 12.

★ Great treasurer, he balanced the books perfectly. The money he owed was exactly the same amount as the money he'd stolen.

★ When there are three burly forwards charging at you, there is only one thing better than presence of mind, and that's absence of body.

★ North Sydney have just won their first premiership in eighty years. Two of their stoutest supporters have celebrated this miracle with the dedication it deserves.

As they stagger home the next day, they accidentally wander into an amusement park and wind up on the roller coaster.

The trip was fast, furious and upside-down. As they staggered off and looked at their surroundings, one was heard to say, 'You know something? We made good time, but I have a feeling we took the wrong bus. Don't you?'

★ One thing I'll say about our club treasurer, he is indeed a very neat man. He's taken this club to the cleaners.

★ Have you ever noticed how a winning dressing-room is always full of hangers on? They are known in the trade as voluntary wharfies.

A voluntary wharfie, of course, is a free-loader.

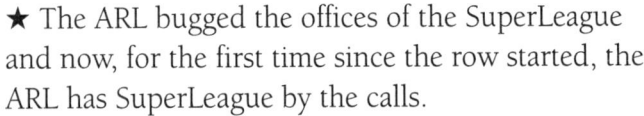

★ The ARL bugged the offices of the SuperLeague and now, for the first time since the row started, the ARL has SuperLeague by the calls.

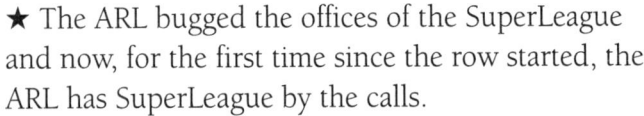

★ John Ribot, the head of SuperLeague, was told there were two visitors waiting to see him.

'Who are they?' asked Ribbon.

'Rupert Murdoch and the Pope,' says his secretary.

'Well, show in the Pope. I only have to kiss his ring.'

★ The Broncos were playing in an away game and the coach had imposed the curfew—back in the hotel by 11.30 p.m.

The first player lobbed in at 1 a.m., and the coach was furious. 'Why are you late?' he said through clenched teeth.

'Well, coach,' said the latecomer, 'I tried to hail a taxi but they were all busy, so I saw this guy with a horse and cart and I offered him $20 to give me a lift. Well coach, you wouldn't believe it—we were halfway up the hill and the horse drops dead, and I had to walk the rest of the way.'

The coach is now seeing red. 'You stupid moron, do you expect me to believe such a cock and bull story? I'm recommending you be fined $1000.'

Just then the second player arrived.

'And where have you been?' said the coach.

'Coach, you're not gonna believe this, but I couldn't get a taxi anywhere. I saw this guy with a horse and cart and he offered to give me a lift for $20. Halfway up the hill the horse dropped dead, so I had to walk the rest of the way home!'

Predictably the coach does his block and fines him $2000. But to the coach's amazement yet another player arrives with the same excuse. And then another, and another, until the last player arrives.

The coach is beside himself with rage, veins bulging at the temple.

'I suppose you couldn't get a taxi either?' he fired, steam coming out of his ears.

'Oh no, coach. I got a taxi all right . . . but I couldn't get up the hill for all the dead horses.' Incredible, really!

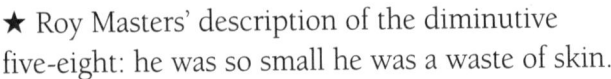

★ Roy Masters' description of the diminutive five-eight: he was so small he was a waste of skin.

★ Show me a gay halfback and I'll show you a passing fancy.

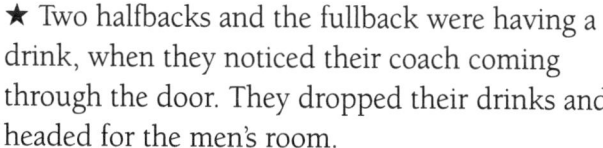

★ Two halfbacks and the fullback were having a drink, when they noticed their coach coming through the door. They dropped their drinks and headed for the men's room.

The barman said to the coach, 'What will you have?'

And the coach said, 'I'll have a beer, and see what the backs in the boys room will have.'

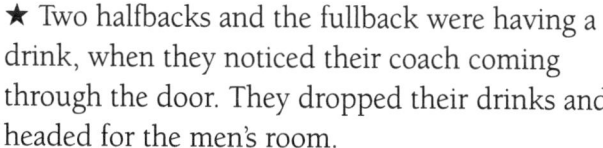

★ Every club a certain footballer in Sydney played for, things would just happen to go missing. He eventually got the nickname 'Batman' because he could do nothing without 'Robin.'

★ That player in question was so crooked they had to screw on his socks.

★ He was the same player who asked a mate of his, 'Did you see the watch the president gave the secretary manager?'

'No,' said the second player, 'show it to me.'

★ It was at the same club where the manager said, 'Listen, I've phoned the police. Every player will have to be searched.'

'Why?'

'Somebody has stolen the goal posts.'

★ Rugby League must be the toughest body contact sport of all. Isn't it wonderful how they determine exactly what position the player will play.

During the pre-season all the players are put in a forest and told to run and run. Those who run at the trees are front row forwards and those who don't are not.

★ There are two great tragedies in Rugby League. One is being asked to appear on the *Footy Show*. The other is actually appearing on it.

★ Pre-season training is where God first got the idea for purgatory.

★ Supervising pre-season training is essential for anyone whose next career move is to be a warden in a Turkish prison.

★ The club hierarchy brought in an efficiency expert. And all he ever said at training was, 'Let the ball do the work.'

He was the kind of kind who would introduce microwaves into crematoriums.

★ Robbo wasn't the brightest footballer in the world. In fact he once sued a bakery for putting his signature on a hot-cross bun.

★ Did you know that . . .

SuperLeague has been approved by the Vatican? They like the way the executive thinks that Mr Murdoch is infallible.

★ A competition was held to pick the score of next year's Grand Final.

The first prize is two tickets to the game!

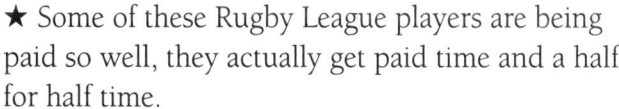

★ Some of these Rugby League players are being paid so well, they actually get paid time and a half for half time.

★ Listen—the Rugby League officials all ganged up on me. You look in the rule book and you'll see that nowhere does it say that a player cannot walk onto the field carrying a baseball bat.

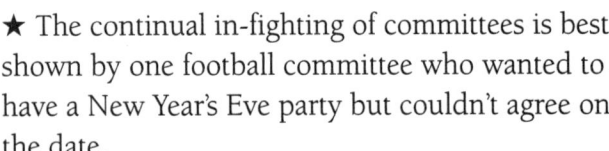

★ I hear your brother went up to Mark Geyer, spat in his eye and called him a wuss.

I'd like to shake his hand.

'You can't—there's a lily in it.'

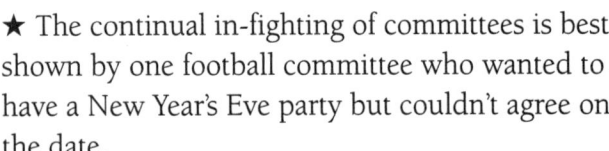

★ The continual in-fighting of committees is best shown by one football committee who wanted to have a New Year's Eve party but couldn't agree on the date.

★ A camel is a horse that was put together by committee.

★ Some of today's players are so pampered that if they cut their leg they don't have it bandaged, they have it gift-wrapped.

★ It is a statistical fact that 99 per cent of all the people that support euthanasia follow the North Sydney Bears.

★ Arthur Beatson, one of the greats if not the greatest of Rugby League's ball-playing forwards, had a reputation for being a good man with a knife and fork. In fact it has been said that if he had been at the Last Supper he would have asked for a doggy bag.

★ Talk about tough: when Blocka Roach tackled you, you forgot the instant replay. All you wanted to see were the X-rays.

★ Being good on the field of play does not necessarily mean you have a great command of the English language. In fact watching your favourite player being interviewed may be quite a letdown.

It's like finding out your interior decorator is colour blind.

★ Dumb: he was the sort of guy who would say to the Godfather, 'Over my dead body.'

★ He's leaving to go to the football, and the annoyed one says, 'Football, football that's all you ever think about. What would happen if when you got there the game was cancelled? And when you came home you found me in bed with the referee, what would you do then?'

'Do? I'll tell you what I'd do—I'd break his white stick and shoot his seeing eye dog!'

★ Tommy Bishop, the great English League and Cronulla halfback caught a lady as she slipped off a railway platform and he quipped, 'This is the first time I've had a fallen woman in my arms.'

Recognising Tommy, she said, 'That's a coincidence because this is also the first time I've been picked up by a Bishop.'

★ The night that the North Sydney Bears win the ARL premiership will be a night to remember.

And why not? They've had nearly eighty years to rehearse for it.

★ The team was not doing well, so as a bonding process the coach organised a fancy dress. The sweet young thing from the office went as a turkey and eleven players went along as sage and onions.

★ He hates to waste anything. If he has to peel onions he will watch North Sydney play at the same time.

★ Front-row forwards like to train in threes. This is because one is able to read, one is able to write, and the third is there to stop these intellectuals becoming fullbacks.

★ The movie *Strictly Ballroom* got its title after the director saw Alfie Langer wearing Artie Beatson's shorts.

★ He had a reputation as a hard drinker. His favourite drink was vodka and cement.

★ Reg Gasnier, one of the all-time legends in Rugby League, retired from playing while in France. On return he was met by a reporter at the airport who said, 'While you were over there did you have any trouble with your French?'

'No,' said Gasnier, 'but the French did.'

★ Nutrition is playing a big part in sport today. The club nutritionist is addressing the players . . . every club has one.

'You are what you eat. As a matter of fact, scientists now think that beer causes cancer,' he revealed.

To which the bright voice from the back responded, 'No problems with me mate, I don't smoke beer.'

★ The timing of the decision to retire from the game is never easy.

'How did you know it was time to retire?' asked the reporter.

'It was simple. One day I was listening to the coach's training and tactics, and I thought I was beginning to see his point of view,' said the player.

★ When asked to describe experience a wise old player in a pensive mood suggested, 'Experience is the comb God gives you when you've lost all your hair.'

★ He was not the brightest recruit. When they told him to sign on the dotted line he went to the circus and tried to rest his contract on the back of a leopard.

★ One year South Sydney lost their first eleven games. In other words, they got the season off to a flying stop.

★ Players become paranoid about their age.
I remember hearing a senior player saying to a raw rookie, 'When I was your age, and incidentally, I am . . .'

★ The politician Bronwyn Bishop is a Parramatta supporter and she was in attendance at the Grand Final when one of her favourite players was stretchered off.

She was so concerned she hurried to the dressing room. 'Were you injured?' she asked.

'Well, let me put it this way,' he replied. 'If you had been injured where I was injured, you wouldn't have been injured at all.'

★ Rugby League is a game where 13 grown men spend 80 minutes trying to move a small object from one end of the ground to the other—a distance of about 100 m.

It was obviously originated by wharfies!

★ Each player read the coach's sixteen-page Grand Final match plan. It is now regarded as the longest suicide note ever written in the history of the club.

★ Have you noticed that the referees in SuperLeague have very, very tight shorts, presumably to appeal to the female spectator? One inch tighter, and they would automatically qualify for the Vienna Boys Choir.

★ I never say to anybody 'Go to Hell'. I just say may you be underweight, undertrained and play for Queensland in the State of Origin Series.

★ Fire broke out in the North Sydney Bears boardroom. The chairman yelled, 'Save the Cups Save the Cups'.

And . . . everybody ran to the canteen.

★ Two fellows had been in Hell for a number of years stoking the fires, when one day they suddenly felt cold air come upon them. Then to their astonishment it started to snow, and all their fires were extinguished and the place became frozen.

'What do you think is going on?' the first men asked in amazement.

'Well,' said the second guy, shaking with the cold, 'I'm only guessing, but something tells me that North Sydney finally won the Grand Final.'

★ He went into John Ribot's office and was surprised to see a telephone on a desk with an earphone but *no* mouthpiece.

'What sort of a phone is that?' he asked.

'Oh,' said the secretary, 'that's Mr Ribot's hotline to Mr Murdoch.'

★ Attila the Hun, Napoleon and John Quale were watching the Russian military parade. Attila looks at the tanks and says, 'If I had tanks like that I could have conquered the whole of Asia.'

Napoleon looks at the ballistic missiles and says, 'With those, I could have ruled the world.'

John Quale looks up from reading his copy of *Pravda* and says 'And if I'd have had a newspaper like this, nobody would have ever heard of SuperLeague.'

★ The effect of watching a lot of sport on commercial television can be seen in the little boy who, in saying his night-time prayers includes the line: 'Give us this day, our daily slow-baked, vitamin-enriched, nourishing, delicious golden brown bread as eaten by Alfie Langer.'

★ Of course you'll see Balmain at the top of the League ladder, but only if you hold the newspaper upside-down.

★ Mark Geyer has been up before the tribunal on numerous occasions.

I didn't think anybody could get into that much trouble and still have their clothes on.

★ Sporting journalist and former coach Roy Masters is not exactly noted for being well dressed. In fact, before his marriage to AFL councillor Elaine Canty, I used to kindly refer to him as a one-man slum.

I am pleased to report that Elaine has improved him beyond recognition. However, in the bad old days, he was leaving Kogarah Oval after a particularly boring game and was met by a St George official who said, 'Roy, look at your suit—it looks as though you sleep in it.'

'Well, since you mention it,' Roy replied, 'I did just wake up.'

★ Isn't nice when the referee and two touch judges are walking on to the field and the band plays 'Three Blind Mice'.

When the team runs out, the band plays 'Send in the Clowns'.

★ The tall poppy syndrome is alive and well in Australia. Let me tell you about the big mouth know-all who, when Johnny Raper was playing, said, 'I think Johnny Raper drinks too much.'

The coach replied, 'Well you find out what he drinks because I'd like to give it to the other twelve players.'

★ How do you make a front row forward laugh after a game?

Well, you tell him a joke before the game.

★ The tall poppy syndrome is when you become so popular that everybody hates you.

★ He was a much travelled player, a Rugby League mercenary. He had played for a lot of clubs. In fact, when he joined his last club, they asked him to sign the visitors' book.

★ Wayne Pearce, that great Balmain and Australian player makes no secret of the fact that he is a health nut and is careful about what he eats. Probably the best dietary advice he ever gave his team was that if you manage to drink a full glass of milk every day for 120 months you will live to be 100!

★ Kenny Arthurson, who did enormous work on behalf of the ARL goes into a bookstore and asks for a copy of the SuperLeague constitution.

'Certainly, Sir,' said the assistant. Then he recognised Ken and said, 'Will I wrap it for you or do you wish to burn it here?'

★ After completing a brain operation the surgeon said to the patient, 'I'm sorry, but we have had to remove 99 per cent of your brain.'

The patient replied, 'Do you know, I think that North Sydney are going to win the League premiership this year.'

★ There have been some great personal rivalries in Rugby League, but thankfully most have stayed on the field. One such rivalry was between Benny Elias and Steve Walters. The story is that Elias comes home from a very hard game, touches a bottle and a genie appears.

The genie says, 'Your wish is my command—any wish you make now will be fulfilled, but remember your fiercest rival will receive the same thing twice over.'

Benny thought for a moment and said, 'I would like one testicle removed.'

★ The Sydney *Footy Show* has done for football what female impersonators have done for Women's Lib.

★ It is a medical fact that for every year you play football in the front row you lose one point off your IQ.

★ The surest way to be alone in sport is to be a front-row forward who is prone to breaking wind.

★ In Rugby League a scrum is a friendship recognised by the police.

★ The Irish forward once got a present of a pair of water skis and went looking for a river with a slope.

★ In the last days of Newtown Leagues Club as a senior team, they lost so many games that one supporter nailed his season's ticket to the club door.

The next day someone had stolen the nail.

★ In the last two years Rugby League has given some average players dramatic increases in salary, which caused one player to say, 'I know I'm living beyond my means, but I can afford it.'

Perhaps it was the same player who, when told by his bank he was $1000 overdrawn, said, 'Don't be stupid. I have not got that much money.'

★ The Irish president comes to God, 'Tell me God, how long will it be before we have peace in Ireland?'

God answered, 'Twenty-five years.'

The Irish president weeps and leaves.

The Israeli president says God, 'How long before we have peace in the Middle East?'

God answered, 'Forty years.'

The Israeli president weeps and leaves.

Next up is the president of North Sydney Football Club. He asks, 'How long, God, before

North Sydney wins a Rugby League Premiership?'
God weeps and leaves.

★ One of the toughest players in the modern era
was Martin Bella. One day somebody fired a gun
at him. The bullet penetrated the bulletproof car, hit
Martin in the forehead, ricocheted and killed
the driver.

★ I once said about St George in a Grand Final that
there was as much chance of them being beaten as
there was of Fred Nile and Bruce Ruxton holding
hands and leading the Mardi Gras.

PS: Brisbane Broncos beat St George in that
game.

PPS: It was like leaving the scene of an accident.

★ He's on top of a building, threatening to jump and the copper says, 'Hold it! Hold it son! Think of all the good things in life. Think of your mother and father.'

The guy says, 'I'm an orphan.'

'Think of your wife or girlfriend.'

'But I'm not married and I haven't got a girlfriend.'

The copper said, 'Well, think of St George winning a grand final.'

The guy said, 'I'm a Manly supporter.'

The copper said, 'Well, jump then, you bastard, jump!'

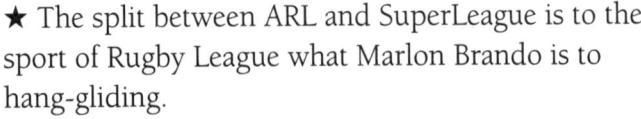

★ The split between ARL and SuperLeague is to the sport of Rugby League what Marlon Brando is to hang-gliding.

★ He became a famous footballer, and made millions of dollars, but he never forgot his parents.

Every week he sent his parents fruit which they sell on the corner of Pitt Street.

★ There's an old saying: 'Two heads are better than one.'

Except of course during a Liverpool kiss.

★ The state Rugby League today, if they did a documentary on it, it would come under the heading of a disaster movie.

STOP . . . the world Rugby League wants to get back on.

★ I once asked ex-Sydney coach Roy Masters (appropriately nicknamed Thirsty), 'What would you do if you had all the money you spent on beer?'

And Roy said, 'I'd buy another beer.' (That was just a joke, Roy.)

★ I had a most unusual experience last week. I went to a Rugby League game and never once heard the home crowd shout, 'Hey Ref, get them back ten metres.'

★ He wasn't that bright really. He thought a spirit level was a breathalyser for carpenters.

★ As he saw the rolled-up lawn being delivered on the back of the truck, he said, 'God, he must be rich. Imagine that—he sends out his lawn to be mowed.'

★ 'He lost $100 on the Grand Final.'

'How come you lost $100? You only bet $50.'

'I know, but we were so unlucky—I bet another $50 on the television replay.'

★ That wonderful sign outside a church: 'If St Peter came back to Earth what would you do?'

Underneath someone had written: 'I'd play him fullback with St George.'

★ You can never beat St George—you can only score more points than them.

★ Front-row forwards in Rugby League are not noted for being intellectual, so it was not surprising when at half-time the coach said, 'You have been playing like pussycats—I want you to go back in there and get ferocious.'

One front-row forward jumped up and said, 'OK coach, what's his number?'

★ A friend of mine supported Newtown League for eleven years, and still didn't know what their victory song was.

★ I remember when Balmain were going through a really bad stage, and they lost their first five games.

But they never got discouraged. They just went back out and lost their next five games.

★ In the dying days of the Newtown Leagues Club first division status—their attendances were bad—a supporter phoned and said, 'What time does the game start?'

To which the official replied, 'What time can you get here?'

★ South are playing North, and it's a typical end-of-season game—both sides out of the semis, nothing at stake . . . hardly a soul at the ground.

A policeman saw two kids climbing over the gate. Unfortunately he was a nasty copper—so he made them go back in and watch the rest of the game.

★ I wonder if this describes any club directors you know: 'He was too busy learning the tricks of the trade to learn the trade itself. But nevertheless he could always be trusted to hit the nail on the thumb.

Unfortunate man—he once grabbed a rattlesnake to kill a stick.

★ I am a St George fan and our supporters are the best in the world—even when we are losing. Last season we lost seven on the trot and we still didn't boo our team. Mind you, it's difficult to boo when you're not even there.

★ St George played a draw with Parramatta in a Grand Final, one of the hardest games on record.

It was so bad that the referee who was mugged when leaving the ground awarded the mugger 'the best and fairest'.

★ It was a simple tactical system: if the captain shouted a word beginning with P such as police or politics, the ball would be kicked to the right and the attack would start from that side of the field.

If he shouted out a word beginning with S, such as singer or suitcase, then the attack came from the left.

But the whole plan fell apart when, one afternoon, the captain yelled, 'Psychology.'

★ Every club hits a bad patch and Parramatta was no exception.

Two kids in the street: 'Let's play Parramatta.'

Second kid says, 'How do you play Parramatta?'

First kid says, 'It's easy. I pass you the ball and you drop it.'

★ After being beaten 60–0 a reporter came up to the coach and said, 'I have three questions to ask you.'

'Who were your best players?'

Coach: 'Didn't have any.'

Reporter: 'How come you let yourselves be beaten 60–0?'

Coach: 'It was a team effort.'

Reporter: 'You obviously drew up the plan—what do you think of the team's execution?'

Coach: 'I'm in favour of it.'

★ A rugby scrum is like a friendship that somehow got out of control.

★ In the recent SuperLeague court case Judge Burchett said, 'No team can play any game that resembles Rugby League.'

The Gold Coast have been doing that for years now!

★ In the State of Origin battle, it's team-mate against team-mate, friend against friend, with no quarter asked or given.

That is why after the game the dressing room is known as a site for sore allies.

★ He was highly qualified in sports management and he was called before the committee for some imaginary indiscretion. For twenty minutes he told the committee how incompetent they were and that they had no right to be running a multi-million dollar enterprise.

Eventually the president rose to his feet and said, 'Now then sonny, there is no need to talk to us like that—we demand some respect. After all, we are all qualified plumbers.'

★ 'Hey coach, what did you think of me today? Ran the length of the field and over the try line.'

'Yes, you stupid dummy,' screams the coach, 'but it only counts if you have the ball.'

'Oh hell,' said the forward. 'Every year new rules.'

★ He says to the sports psychiatrist, 'Doc, I'm worried about the fact that I'm shy, I'm timid and I'm indecisive. It's affecting my social life and it's starting to affect my game.'

The psychiatrist said, 'Don't let it bother you. Certainty is the prerogative of idiots.'

And the player asks, 'Are you sure about that, doctor?'

And the psychiatrist replied, 'I am absolutely certain.'

★ Our team has an unusual drug problem.

Every time we go on the field we get drugged from one end to the other.

★ You know your team is in for a bad season when the coach says he hasn't got the players.

The players say the coach is useless.

Both sides are right.

★ She says I ignore the family during the football season, but that's ridiculous. How could I?

Because at half-time I always make it a point to talk to my wife and two daughters—or is it three?

★ Maybe these were the same two still celebrating a day later when one lifted his glass, skulled his drink and collapsed on the floor. His mate looked at him in total admiration and said, 'That's what I like about him—he knows when to quit.'

★ I think everyone should follow a football team. I think at one stage in our life it is our God-given right to be able to stand tall on the terrace and shout 'These bastards can't play.'

★ Brad Fittler, the Australian Captain, is one of the new breed of very wealthy sportsmen.

In fact, when his car needed a new horn, he hired music legend James Morrison.

★ Johnny 'Chook' Raper, arguably the best player ever to play for St George or for that matter Australia, arrives at the gates of heaven.

The angel says, 'Chook, Did you do anything bad in your life?'

And Chook says, 'I drank too much. As a young man I played up a bit. When I played football I did pull the occasional illegal trick to win.'

And the angel says, 'Go straight into Heaven.'

A surprised Raper says, 'Thanks very much, St Peter.'

The angel says, 'I'm not St Peter.'

He said, 'Well who are you?'

And the angel said, 'St George.'

★ Ray Hadlee, the great football caller on 2UE, at one stage was calling 3 to 4 games a week and filling in for John Laws on the morning program. No wonder he phoned up his doctor and said, 'Hey Doc, can a tongue get a hernia?'

★ Before he was married a certain Australian League captain made love to his partner six times within the hour, and amazed some of Australia's top doctors. They were sitting at the next table.

★ You can always tell a talkative taxi driver. He has a statue of Ray Hadlee on his dashboard.

★ Kevin Ryan, the great St George forward who later became a barrister and a member of the NSW Parliament, was by reputation the toughest player to play League.

But there is no truth in the rumour that when he made a good tackle his coach rewarded him by throwing him a piece of raw meat.

★ Ray Warren once mentioned that he was the second-best Rugby League umpire in the nation.

I asked him 'Who do you think is the best?'

'All the other umpires tied for first.'

★ Clive Churchill, one of Rugby League's immortals—and one of the greatest full backs of all time, once said that blind people went to the game just to hear him kick the ball.

★ When I asked Rex Mossop, the Manly and Australian dual international player, if he missed playing football, he thought for a moment and said, 'Brian, I even miss the injuries.'

★ Bob Carr, Premier of NSW, is quite notorious for his lack of interest in sport, so maybe the following story is true.

'Mr Premier, I'd like you to meet Jason Taylor. He plays with the Bears.'

'Oh good, I've always liked animal acts.'

★ 'I hear the supporters' club is looking for a new treasurer.'

'I thought they'd just elected one last month.'

'We did—he's the one we're looking for.'

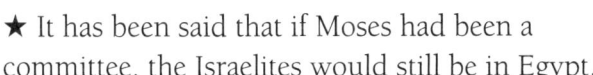

★ It has been said that if Moses had been a committee, the Israelites would still be in Egypt.

★ If a sufficient number of committees are placed on top of each other it can be assured that disaster is not left to chance.

Rugby Union

★The casualty ward on a Saturday night is the living proof we still play Rugby Union.

—Brian Doyle

★ As a coach he spends half of his time telling the press what his team is going to do, and the other half explaining why they haven't done it.

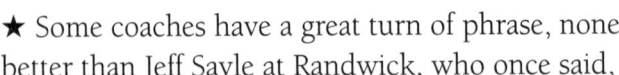

★ The Rugby Union supporter walking along the beach at Bondi finds a bottle. He rubs the bottle and the genie appears.

'Your wish is my command,' he says.

And the young supporter says, 'I want to be as fast as David Campese, as good a player a Mark Ella, and as great a captain as Nick Farr-Jones.'

And the genie says, 'I think you'd better put me back in the bottle.'

★ Some coaches have a great turn of phrase, none better than Jeff Sayle at Randwick, who once said,

'The player was so bad he was about as useful as a chocolate teapot.'

★ Or, as he said to another player, 'If you really liked this club, you would have played for someone else.'

★ It was that sort of game—a bit of booing, a lot of clapping and then you realised they were clapping the booing.

★ The Union players' lament: 'If only our coach was as well known as his methods'.

★ 'You want to get on with the coach? I'll give you the secret. When he's giving us a talk, object to every second thing he says.'

'Why do that?'

'It makes him think you're listening.'

★ 'He was my second choice as captain.'

'Well, who was your first choice?'

'Anybody else.'

★ 'Of course you are essential to the team. It's players who play as badly as you who make the others look good.'

★ Coach: 'I had a great dream last night—a beautiful girl came into my room, naked, with her 16 stone, 7 foot brother who could run the hundred metres in 9 seconds.'

★ 'My wife is my best friend and my severest critic.'

'Well,' said his mate, 'your severest critic is in your bedroom, and your best friend just jumped out the window.'

★ I knew Rugby Union was a tough game after my first tackle.

Three of them got me: one grabbed the right leg, one grabbed the left leg and the third said, 'Right lads, let's make a wish.'

★ Jeff Sayle tells how he was asked to speak at a Rugby dinner in the bush and, rather than accept the small fee, he suggested that they donate it to charity.

The president said, 'That's very kind of you Jeff, would you mind if we donated it to our special fund?'

And Jeff said 'Certainly, whatever you want. What's your special fund anyway?'

'Well', the president said, 'we're saving up to get better speakers next year.'

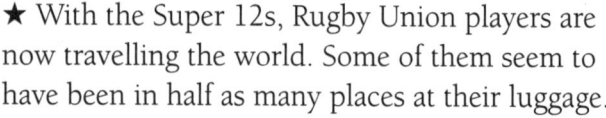

★ With the Super 12s, Rugby Union players are now travelling the world. Some of them seem to have been in half as many places at their luggage.

★ Every skill I have I owe to my coach, and despite that, my lawyers think I have no case.

★ The new best-seller is called *Everything you wanted to know about Rugby but were afraid to ask the bloke in the stand who never played the game.*

★ Drinking is part of the culture of Rugby Union. Unfortunately our captain was run over by a brewery truck.

We reckon it was the first time in years that the drinks were on him.

★ He was by far the most famous player that this small town had produced. He was also the most generous, so much so that he considered it an insult if any of the townspeople bought him a drink.

However, being the sensible lad he was, he learnt to swallow all his insults.

★ You watch them play and realise that not all the ding-a-lings are on the Mr Whippy trucks.

★ Before every game the coach was known to give the same motivational speech. I think he was studying to be a xerox machine.

★ Alan Jones not only coached Australia in Rugby Union, he's also one of the greats in radio, and without a doubt, one of the best motivational speakers you have ever heard.

Perhaps that was the reason when one of his players fainted and Jonesy gave him motivational-to-motivational resuscitation.

★ I once said to Alan Jones about a certain player, 'Does he answer all his fan letters?'

And Jones said 'How could he? He barely has time to write them.'

★ They had just toured England, Ireland, Scotland and Wales, and as the team was getting on the plane to come back to Sydney the manager said,

'Gentlemen, this is my last speech to you. As you all know, the enemies of all professional sports people are booze and fast ladies. Today I must congratulate you on the way you have learnt to love your enemies.'

★ 'Hey coach, if you get concussed how long can you play after your brain stops functioning?'

The coach: 'I don't know. How old are you?'

★ Football committees are an IQ unto themselves.

They have been described as a collection of the unfit chosen from the unwilling by the incompetent to do the unnecessary.

★ Jonah Lomu, big man, great footballer has a ferocious tackling technique—he's one step ahead of breaking and entering.

★ Overheard at the Catholic Schools' game: 'There's our skipper. You've heard of the rambling wreck from Melbourne Tech, well, here's the total loss from Holy Cross.'

★ An hour before the game, the coach receives a phone call.

'Sorry, coach, I can't play today. My wife broke a leg.'

'What's that got to do with you playing?'

'Well, it was my leg she broke!'

★ It's a kind of Irish excuse he gave the tribunal for breaking the scrum half's jaw: 'I have no idea how it happened, I had nothing in my hand when I hit him . . . except my fist.'

★ The star—the boy from the bush—goes to the city for a trial, and after a few days he sends home a fax: 'Made the third team, now that's a feather in my cap.'

Another few weeks go by. He sends a second fax: 'Made the second team, another feather in my cap.'

A month goes by, and the family receives a third fax: 'Another feather in my cap. I'm playing for the firsts team this week.'

Obviously it couldn't last, and the next fax read: 'Coach said I'm a big head and sacked me—send money for fare home.'

To which his father faxed back: 'Use feathers and fly.'

★ He had a chequered career in football—as a player he had all the impact of a streaker in a nudist camp.

★ As a referee he was as popular as a father's day speech in a home for unmarried mothers.

★ When he took up coaching he was so very class conscious—he didn't have any class and he was so very conscious of it.

★ Coach watching a new player training: 'If he is the answer to a coach's prayer, I don't think God was paying much attention.'

★ As a player he believes determination is the key to success. He makes a point of finishing something every day of his life.

Most days it's a six-pack.

★ He visited the club psychiatrist because he was very short and very insecure about his height.

The psychiatrist reminded him that not only were some of the great players in the game small, but so were some of the great figures of world history: Napoleon, Toulouse-Lautrec, Sir Gordon Richards.

The little guy left the club psychiatrist feeling completely cured.

On the way home a dog ate him.

★ During the first training session of the season the trainer said, 'Remember your body is your home, so keep it clean and neat.'

To which one of the players replied, 'You're quite right. I have a woman, and she comes twice a week.'

★ The honour of this club is at stake with this game, so we must do one of three things: win, draw or protest.

★ Maybe that was the team that did a lap of honour when they won the toss.

★ 'How badly did we play?'

'We were beaten 45–0 and we were lucky to get nil.'

★ That was at the time when a disgruntled supporter said, 'They must be on drugs.'

At which the coach replied, 'Well, it couldn't be speed.'

★ He was retiring from the game, and like so many before him, money was now a problem. Then it dawned on him that the people who had sponsored his club were all foreign car dealers or manufacturers.

So he found the magic lamp, rubbed it and the genie appeared, 'You have one wish, Sir.'

He said, 'Foreign car dealers are making all the money. I wish to be a foreign car dealer in a major city.'

And that was how he became a Rolls Royce dealer in Sarajevo.

★ Players' reunion. He had drunk his share, your share and my share, and the brewery reserve.

Eventually he said, 'I want to get home.'

He got to the door of the hotel and said to the doorman, 'Call me a cab.'

The man at the door said, 'My good chap, I am not a doorman. I'm an admiral in Her Majesty's Navy.'

'OK, call me a boat, I still want to get home.'

★ 'Of course I do my exercises at home, coach. Every morning—45 minutes of exercise.

'Some mornings I do them so fast it only takes me 10 minutes.'

★ He was the kind of player you'd expect to see emerging from a scrum with the remains of a jockstrap between his teeth.

★ I once saw a T-shirt that said: Give Blood—Play Rugby.

★ He says to his trainer, 'Why is it when I stand on my head all my blood rushes to my head, but when I stand on my feet my blood doesn't rush to my feet?'

'Because,' said the trainer, 'your feet are not empty.'

★ He addressed the team after their ninth defeat and said, 'Don't worry lads, things are going to get a lot worse before they get worse.'

★ He was probably the same coach who laughs all the way to his Valium bottle.

★ It was the only club that had *Custer's Last Stand* as a training film.

★ They had had so many rorts in club elections over the previous years that when the president was defeated, everybody was astonished. The ex-president, of course, complained, saying he was a victim.

'A victim of what?' asked a member.

'A victim of accurate counting,' replied the new president.

★ He played so much Rugby at school that he didn't pass one exam. In fact the ultimate disgrace came when he failed bingo.

★ Two Irish priests were watching Ireland play England.

'You know,' said the first priest, 'Union really is the game they play in Heaven. It is a game of skilled sportsmanship and above all, character-building. Here we are, watching a game between us and the old enemy. The important thing is not who wins or who loses, but how the game is played.

'Providing, of course, we beat the Pommy bastards.'

★ As a coach he had no equals, only superiors.

★ The logic of coaching: 'Remember son, you are now the assistant coach. By working hard eight hours a day you'll eventually rise to be the club coach like me, and work twelve hours a day.'

★ The nineteen-year-old know-all is trying very hard to put one over the fifty-year-old coach, who becomes so exasperated he said, 'Listen son, don't try to be smart with me. I was in uniform when you were in liquid form.'

★ In sport it takes two people to really hurt you: the selector who dropped you, and the coach who tells you why.

★ The trainer is getting angrier by the minute at the players' inability to form a straight line across the field. He screamed at them, 'Do you call that a straight line? Just fall out and have a look at it!'

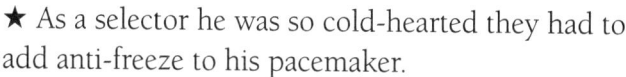

★ Sports psychologists today are very much a part of big-time sports, and he is having a one-to-one with the club's newest recruit.

'You tell me you are not indecisive and have no trouble making up your mind. Well, I ask you one question: when you get the ball in a fullback position, do you know exactly what to do?'

'Well, yes and no.'

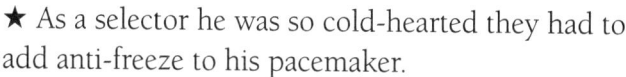

★ As a selector he was so cold-hearted they had to add anti-freeze to his pacemaker.

★ The difference between the board of certain football clubs and a kindergarten is that the kindergarten has adult supervision.

★ The coach is interviewing a player who has been signed by the football committee.

'What's your IQ?'

'Perfect,' he replied, '20–20.'

★ The front row hits back.

'What's dumber than a dumb front rower?'

'A smart fullback.'

★ I'm not sure what position he played. He was either a fullback or a drawback.

★ He arrived at the gates of Heaven.

St Peter said, 'What was your main claim to fame on Earth?'

'Well, in front of 40,000 people at Ballymore I crossed the try line for Australia against England, only to drop the ball.'

St Peter said, 'When was that?'

'About 2 minutes ago.'

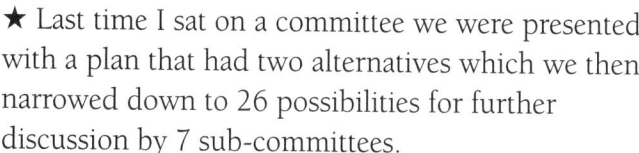

★ Last time I sat on a committee we were presented with a plan that had two alternatives which we then narrowed down to 26 possibilities for further discussion by 7 sub-committees.

★ He had played in the golden oldies, and now every bone in his body was telling him he was an idiot. He turned to his son and said, 'I don't think there is anything worse than being old and bent.'

And the son said, 'How about being young and broke?'

★ The newspaper report said the team played bad, but that was only because there wasn't enough space to say fucking awful.

★ I am not a know-all selector—it's just that a number of ill-informed people disagree with me.

★ 'I'd like to speak to the landlord of the club house.'

'Speaking.'

'It's about the roof.'

'What about it?'

'We'd like one.'

★ The cleverest description of a club director:
Power with a Lobotomy.

★ Where's the treasurer?'

'Didn't you hear? The committee accused him of stealing.'

'Did he leave in a huff?'

'No, in a Rolls Royce.'

★ It was that sort of a club—they had a problem for every solution.

★ Let me tell you how well the club was going.

The accounts department had a rubber stamp marked paid and it was three months before anybody knew it was missing.

★ The trouble with our president is that he runs out of ideas long before he runs out of words.

★ Our club's marketing department could not sell binoculars if Sharon Stone was doing a streak.

★ It wasn't a big club, but they had a chairman of the board, a deputy chairman, a treasurer, praise coordinator, press coordinator, new membership manager and merchandising chef.

His name was George.

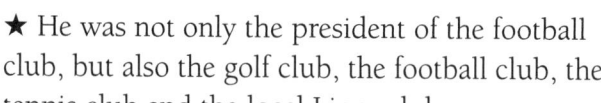

★ He was not only the president of the football club, but also the golf club, the football club, the tennis club and the local Lions club.

In fact it can rightly be said he had a wide range of ignorance.

★ We were the only club with a 'Ways and Dreams' committee.

Soccer

★One of the saddest things about being a professional soccer coach is that your livelihood depends on eleven people—half of whom you wouldn't invite home for dinner.

Attributed to Sir Alf Ramsey, England's World Cup winning coach

★ The average British migrant has very little affiliation to any Australian soccer club. To him it is the unspellables against the unpronounceable.

★ My problem as the manager is that I don't have a good centre forward.

If I had a good centre forward, I'd have a great forward line—providing I had another four good forwards.

★ The coach turned on the centre forward and said, 'That is the worst game you have ever played. If you play like that next week my father will turn over in his grave.'

The centre forward said, 'But your father is still alive.'

The coach said, 'Well, today's game will probably kill him.'

★ I'll tell you how bad the crowds are—the supporters who have never come have stopped coming.

★ It was a small crowd. In fact the Queen would have had more people in her bedroom.

★ For years he sat on the reserves bench, never got a game. Then one day at training the coach singles him out and says, 'It's nil all, there's 30 seconds to go. We are awarded the penalty and our two penalty takers are injured. What would you do?'

'Ah, well coach', stammered the nervous reserve. 'I'd slide down to the end of the bench so as I could get a better view.'

★ I played in a pub team and we didn't win for two years. However, people said we were great losers.

But that wasn't true. We weren't great losers, we were *perfect* losers.

★ I'll tell you how good the team I coached was. Last season we practised by positioning 11 dustbins in the field and we practised passing and dribbling.

The dustbins beat us 6–nil.

★ The centre forward was so conceited he jumped up to head the ball and his head got caught between the posts.

★ He went out to see his local team play a night game and came home ten years later.

His wife said, 'Well what have you got to say for yourself?'

He said, 'We lost 2–nil.'

She said, 'Well, sit down and don't blame me if your tea is cold.'

★ In ten games the club had played him in about nine positions, from goal keeper to outside right. In fact it was said that he had been tried everywhere except in the Supreme Court.

★ Soccer manager went into hospital for a nervous breakdown. He was only in there three days and he had one.

★ The soccer club, Fairfield Marconi, and David Hill, the chief of Soccer Australia get on like brothers—Cain and Abel.

★ He was new to the game of soccer so they played him in the forwards. He didn't score, but in the first fifteen minutes he hit the cross-bar eight times.

Later they took 47 splinters out of his forehead.

★ What a club this would be if we could just teach the players how to talk and the coach how to listen.

★ Little kid comes home from playing in the Under Sevens.

His dad says, 'How did you do?'

He said, 'We won 110–4.'

'You scored 110 goals? What was the other goal keeper doing?'

'Well, most of the time he was crying.'

★ 'Did we play bad?'

'Bad? Bad?! I'll tell you how bad we played! In our team a pedestrian would have been someone in a hurry.'

★ The president of the Wagga Wagga Rovers Soccer Club went to the annual meeting of FIFA, the World Soccer body. When he got there he was most annoyed that nobody had ever heard of Wagga Wagga Rovers.

'Back home in Australia', he told the meeting, 'we are world famous.'

★ The manager is giving the pre-match instructions.

'And above all,' he said, 'all penalties are to be taken by Brown, the centre forward.'

Sure enough, with one minute to go the score is 2–2. They get a penalty shot.

The goalkeeper races up, places the ball, takes the penalty and misses. The final whistle blows.

The manager rushes up, 'I said Brown was to take the penalties. Is your name Brown?'

He said, 'No boss, my name is Green.'

He said, 'Well, why then did you take the

penalty? Are you deaf or just stupid?'

'No boss, just colour blind.'

★ As the man said, 'If this team profits by its mistakes, we'll have one hell of a season ahead of us.'

★ 'This is the worst season I've ever had,' said the soccer manager.

'My wife keeps telling me to leave my troubles at the club. If I left my troubles at the club I wouldn't be able to see the ground.'

★ I was a very minor soccer club official. In fact, if they wanted to teach anybody about our club from the ground up, they started with my job.

★ The team was so slow that at one stage it had to speed up just to stop.

★ They say a coach's job is finished when his players walk out of the tunnel. That is probably true because during a game a coach controls his team like a barometer controls the weather.

★ He was one of those Latin American temperamental players: 50 per cent temper, 50 per cent mental.

★ As the player says to the coach, 'Nobody in the team talks to me.'

The coach says, 'Next.'

★ The only good thing about being manager of a soccer club is that you get to fool around with the manager's wife.

★ The coach was at the end of his tether: 'You have done everything wrong,' he screamed.

'Let us now have some honesty. If there is anyone here who thinks he is responsible for us being at the bottom of the ladder, would he please stand up.'

Eventually one soul stood up.

The coach sneered, 'So, you think you are responsible for our failure?'

'Well, not really coach I just didn't want to see you standing up there on your own.'

★ I'll tell you how bad we were—just before kick-off, our captain said a prayer and a voice said, 'Forget it. I only do miracles on Tuesdays and Thursdays.'

★ We were a bad team. When we played, the ball came with instructions.

★ As a soccer player I was as successful as Marcel Marceau on radio.

★ It was raining cats and dogs, and after he'd won the toss, the captain said to the umpire, 'Do we have to play in this rain?'

'Yes,' came the unpleasant reply. 'Now which end do you want?'

'Well,' said the captain, 'if it's all the same to you, we'll kick with the tide.'

★ 'What's the size of this club?' said the newcomer.

And the boy said, 'Five foot two.'

He said, 'You idiot, what do you mean five foot two?'

'Well,' he said, 'my dad is six foot tall and every time we lose he puts his hand up to his chin and says "I've had this club up to here."'

★ He went out with an umpire's daughter and got penalised three times. Once for interference, once for handling, and once for trying to pull her jersey off.

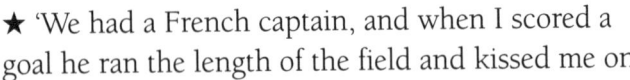

★ The coach called the Little Leaguer to the sideline.

'Now listen, Jimmy, you know the principles of good sportsmanship that Little League tries to promote. No shouting at the umpires, no abusing opponents, no displays of bad temper. You understand what I'm saying?'

'Yes, sir.'

'Well Jimmy, would you please explain it to your mother?'

★ 'We had a French captain, and when I scored a goal he ran the length of the field and kissed me on both cheeks.'

'What did you do?'

'What else could I do—I married him!'

★ He was exceptionally dumb so the coach made him captain for the day, hoping to inspire him. He won the toss, but didn't know what decision to make.

He raced over to the dug-out, 'Coach, nobody will tell me what to do.'

The coach said, 'You have one hope—go back to the umpire and ask him to toss again and maybe this time you'll lose.'

★ It was a really torrid local derby. And both players were giving it not only to each other but also to the umpire.

Eventually there was a mid-field collision and the umpire said, 'Free kick.'

And both captains crowded in around him and said, 'Who for?'

And the referee said, 'Us.'

★ The West Indians have a very distinct accent. So when their manager told their soccer team, 'I want everyone in defence', it was not surprising when they all rushed off the ground and stuck their heads in the railings.

★ I'll tell you how bad we played . . . we couldn't even score a goal at half-time.

★ The umpire had been giving the player a bad time, and eventually he gives him a yellow card.

The player said, 'I suppose if I called you a stupid bastard you'd send me off?'

'Of course I would', said the umpire.

'If I only thought you were a stupid bastard, you couldn't do anything then, could you?'

'No, I don't suppose I could,' said the umpire.

'Well, in that case, I think you are stupid bastard.'

★ He sent in five dollars conscience money to his local football club. They sent him back a letter asking which player he wanted to buy.

★ He was such a bad goalkeeper that when the plane was crashing, he went to put his head between his knees and missed.

★ On a noticeboard of a dressing-room on her first day on the job as the club physiotherapist.

'In case of any strain or groin injury, please contact first thing Monday our physiotherapist Joan McSweeney.'

Underneath someone had written, 'She'll kiss it and make it better.'

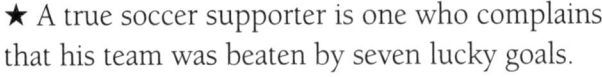

★ A true soccer supporter is one who complains that his team was beaten by seven lucky goals.

★ In World Cup soccer a country can claim any player whose parents or even grandparents were born in that country, or if the player himself has migrated to that country.

Australia has taken full advantage of this.

In fact, it is said that a real soccer fan is one who knows the nationality of every member of the Australian soccer team.

★ It is no secret in soccer circles that David Hill and the ex-president of Marconi Club are not great friends. But what is not too well known is that at David's birthday the ex-president gave him a present of a microwave oven . . . and told him it was a hair-drier!

★ Ron Barassi once saved Australian Soccer coach Frank Arok from drowning. As he dragged him onto the river bank Frank gasped, 'Thank you Ron, but I want to retain the respect of my players. Please don't tell them that I can't swim.'

Ron replied, 'Certainly, Frank . . . if you don't tell my players that I can't walk on water!'

★ The president said to the coach, 'I think I've found a couple of players good enough to play for us.'

To which the coach replied, 'We have enough players good enough to play for us. What we need are a few good enough to play for Manchester United.'

★ Forget the World Cup. The next nuclear war will be held in Melbourne, so that Australia doesn't have to qualify.

Horses and Gambling

★It's a tough race to pick
... there are more tips
than a tin of asparagus.

—*John Tapp, the best race-caller in the business*

★ My favourite racehorse story is about the owner who had a dream and saw his horse win the Melbourne Cup. The horse was a rank outsider at 300–1.

But the owner was adamant, 'I saw him win by ten lengths. I saw it clearly right down to the dirt on the jockey's face and the black armband he was wearing.'

And the race turned out exactly how the owner had described: the horse won by ten lengths and the jockey even wore a black armband. Which explains why the owner never collected his bet. He died the day before.

★ There is obviously a lot of competition among horse trainers.

In fact, as one trainer remarked, 'The only time all the trainers get together is for another trainer's funeral . . . and that's just to get the horses off the widow.'

★ 'Who were you talking to?'

'Tipster. He wanted to give me the winner of the Melbourne Cup.'

'Did you take it?'

'Nah, we've only got a very small garden.'

★ 'My daddy's very kind to animals', I keep hearing him say.

'If only I could get that bastard who keeps scratching horses.'

★ The owner was furious and said to the jockey, 'Why didn't you go for the gap that opened up 600 m from the post?'

The jockey looked at him wearily and said, 'Did you ever try to go for a gap that was going faster than your horse?'

★ Man to his mate at the racecourse: 'I'm sorry George, I've got no money to bet. My wife blew it all on food and rent.'

★ Same man to his mate: 'Every time I come home from a race meeting, while I'm asleep, my wife goes through my pockets, and that really makes me angry.'

'Why should that make you so angry?'

'She never finds anything.'

★ It was an affectionate race—the jockey held his hands around the horse's neck, the horse hooked the rails, and I kissed my money good-bye.

★ You know your horse is slow when, after the race, you have to pay your jockey time and a half.

★ 'Doctor, I have a problem. I think I'm a horse.'

Doctor says, 'I think I can cure you, but it will cost you a lot of money.'

'Oh, money's no problem, Doc, I just won the Melbourne Cup.'

★ I've always liked the one where he was stopped driving a horse's float that was empty. He said he was taking the scratchings.

★ Two horses finished behind my horse. Unfortunately they were first and second in the next race.

★ I follow the horses. Unfortunately the horses I follow also follow the horses.

★ How do you stop a runaway horse?
   Easy, you just put money on it.

★ He says to the bookie, 'My wife over there, you see her in the red dress—well, she's a bit odd. Bets a lot, but likes to pay you in bottle tops. So if you just tolerate her, at the end of the meeting I'll come and settle up.'

The bookie agrees reluctantly, but he agrees.

And at the end of the race the husband comes over and says, 'How much do I owe you?'

And the bookie says, '$1125.'

'No problem,' says the husband. 'Do you have change of this dustbin lid?'

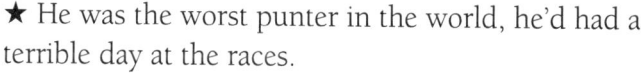

★ He was the worst punter in the world, he'd had a terrible day at the races.

So, very desperate, late that night he broke into the TAB and lost another $100.

★ First time in a greyhound meeting. His mates gee him up, and tell him to back the hare. Now, the bookie, who is no fool, accepts the bet.

Obviously the hare finished first, so he goes straight up to the bookie to collect his winnings.

The bookie says, 'I'm sorry, I can't pay you.'

He says, 'Why not? The hare won!'

The bookie says, 'Listen, I know the hare won, you know the hare won, the spectators know the hare won, the hare knows it won, but that stupid judge has given it to No. 5.'

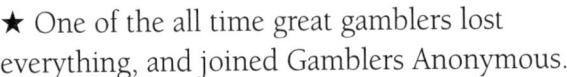

★ One of the all time great gamblers lost everything, and joined Gamblers Anonymous.

And the first thing he did was bet on how long it would take for him to give up gambling.

★ The show-jumping couple who were arrested for making love near the water-jump asked for ten other fences to be taken into consideration.

★ It was at the first bend on the Melbourne Cup. Three horses collide and their jockeys are thrown to the ground. One has a broken arm, broken leg and a dislocated collarbone, but in an amazing display of courage, he remounts the horse and races the most memorable race of all time.

The thousands at Flemington, the millions watching on television watched in awe as he was first past the post. The crowd erupted in a noise equal to a rocket launch.

With cheers ringing in his ears, he failed to hear the trainer say, 'You stupid bastard, you remounted the wrong horse.'

★ This greyhound had lost every race, every single race. Until someone said to the owner, 'You know what will improve that dog? Put some lead in his left ear.'

The owner said, 'How could I do that?'

His friend said, 'With a gun.'

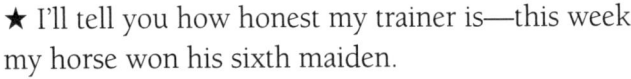

★ I'll tell you how honest my trainer is—this week my horse won his sixth maiden.

★ The jockey was under instructions to lose the race, which he did.

After the race the owner said, 'I was a bit worried. You had that whip going all the time.'

The jockey said, 'You were worried? I was worried myself because once or twice I nearly hit the horse.'

★ Have you noticed how often the TAB has six windows and just two tellers?

Do you think it's their way of saying 3–1 you don't get your money back?

★ The TAB is a place where windows clean people.

★ Casey and Murphy went to the races. First race, they decided Bushtown Boy was going to win, so Casey went down to place the bets on for both of them.

When he came back he said, 'Listen, I met this guy and he says he knows the owner. Bushtown Boy hasn't got a hope. Snowgirl is a certainty, so I put the money on Snowgirl.'

Well, Snowgirl finished stone motherless last.

Next race they decide, The Judge. Casey goes down to place the bets and comes back saying the same thing. 'I met this guy again. He convinced me Falconer was the horse to back.'

And needless to say, Falconer finishes out of the money. The same thing happens the whole afternoon, so the last race is over and they've $5 between them and Murphy says, 'We may as well have a drink before we go, I'll have a Foster's.'

Casey goes to the bar and comes back with two half whiskies.

'I said I wanted a Foster's,' shouts Murphy.

And Casey said, 'I met the same tipster again.'

★ The trainer phoned up the owner and said, 'I'm terribly sorry, sir, but your horse just fell dead.'

And the owner said, 'I don't understand. He's never done that before.'

★ He's at the track and says to his mate, 'I've got a sign. For three nights now, I've dreamt about salami, pastrami and corned beef, and look, on the next race, three horses—believe it or not Salami, Pastrami and Corned Beef. I'm going to back the three of them.'

Which he did, and unfortunately for him, the race was won by an outsider called 'Cold Cuts'.

★ He came home from the races wearing a yachting cap, and his wife said, 'How did you do?

He said, 'With what I won I bought this yachting cap.'

What he forgot to say was that, with what he lost he could have bought the yacht.

★ The horse was so slow the jockey kept a diary. Or was it a calendar?

★ Brendan and Desmond were both dedicated punters, but only Brendan ever made any money— every week Desmond did his.

He finally asked Brendan his secret. 'Well, Desmond, I don't really have a system but opposite the front of the racecourse is a little church and I always go there before I bet and I light a dollar candle in front of the statue of St Jude—the patron saint of hopeless causes—and it doesn't matter what I bet, it always seems to win.'

Desmond follows this advice but as usual, does his dough, so he phones Brendan. 'Were you kidding me? I did what you suggested and I still did my money.'

Brendan says, 'Well, that's weird. You went in to that little church opposite the racecourse?'

'I did.'

'And you lit a one dollar candle in front of the statue of St Jude?'

'Well nearly, I couldn't get a one dollar candle so I lit two fifty-cent candles.'

'Oh you idiot', said Brendan, 'you used the small candles—they are only for the greyhounds.'

★ 'He looks so depressed', he says to the horse trainer. 'What are you thinking about?'

The horse trainer said, 'It's my future.'

'Well, what makes it so hopeless?'

'My past,' was the reply.

★ You work this one out: he needed $500 to pay off his bookie and he only had $400, so he took the

$400 to a pawn shop and pawned it for $300 and sold his pawn ticket to a passer-by for $200 and paid the bookie the $500.

★ The box-office cashier phones the manager: 'There are two racehorses in the theatre foyers.'

Manager: 'What do they want?'

Cashier: 'Two stalls for the Saturday matinee.'

★ Octagonal retired at the age of four. That's what I call a superannuation plan. He now gets approximately $30,000 a time in stud fees at approximately 100 times a year.

That's what I call a retirement.

★ He entered the eight-year-old horse in his first race, and obviously never having run before, the horse was 100–1. Well, the horse was greased lightning, and won by thirty lengths.

The stewards were naturally suspicious and the owner was brought before them.

'How come you've never raced this horse before—after all, you've had it for eight years?'

'Well, to be honest,' said the owner, 'we couldn't catch him until he was seven.'

★ What a horse! If his parents could see him they'd turn over in their glue bottles.

★ What about the short-sighted jockey who couldn't find the weigh-in . . .

★ If horse-racing is the sport of Kings, is drag-racing the sport of Queens?

★ Two priests, both desperate punters, had not had a winner all day. On the last race, they decide on the same horse, and to give it a better chance, the first priest offers his praise to heaven.

'Holy father, heavenly grace—may Shane Dye win this race.'

The second priest too asks for a little help, 'Holy father up in heaven, may Shane Dye come in at 100–7.'

Well, the race commentator whose box was just above them heard all this and after 'They're off', the race commentator began. 'This is the voice of the holy ghost. Shane Dye has been left at the post.'

★ The police had a disappointing day today acting on information received—it finished a bad fourth!

★ It was the hottest day of the year without a doubt. The greyhound was chasing the hare and they were both walking.

★ After an afternoon at the track, the punter said, 'I broke even, thank God. I really needed the money!'

★ He went to the track with no money so he just bet mentally. By the sixth race he'd lost his mind.

'I'm training a greyhound now. God, he's such a lovely dog, he's just like one of the family.'

'I know,' said his mate, 'I can see the resemblance.'

★ The new jockey sensation denied he was romantically involved with the young actress of the moment, saying, 'We have nothing in common. She's interested in boys and I'm interested in girls.'

★ 'I don't understand Bert, he loses so much on horses yet he is lucky playing poker.'

The second guy says, 'Let him shuffle the horses.'

★ Good horse—there he is, racing for the line, driving all the other horses in front of him.

★ He was horse-racing mad, so much so that when his wife gave birth to triplets he named them Win, Place and Also Ran.

★ The psychologist had just finished his lecture and was taking questions.

'Did you say that a good gambler is so disciplined that he could hold down any job?'

'Yes I did,' said the psychologist. 'Do you dispute that?'

'Yes I do', said the man. 'Why would a good gambler need a job?'

★ I had a bit of luck at the races the other day.

I went to Flemington and it was packed.

As I said, I had a bit of luck . . . for the first four races I couldn't get to a bookie!

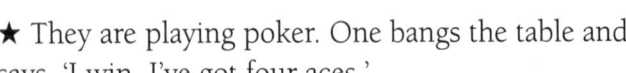

★ I've worked it out: the only way to make money at the race track is to forget about picking horses, and start picking pockets.

And if you've only got one finger you can pick lifesavers.

But if the truth be known, the only people who make money following the horses are the ones who follow with a bucket and a shovel.

★ They are playing poker. One bangs the table and says, 'I win, I've got four aces.'

And the second guy says, 'I'm sorry, but I win.'
First guy: 'But that's impossible, what have you got?'
And he said, 'A gun!'

★ He had a massive heartache at his usual Friday night poker game, and died.

Out of respect his fellow players finished the hand standing up.

★ Doctors say that sex after a big game is relaxing. However my wife says that doesn't apply to Tuesday-night Bingo.

★ Q: How do you tell a moron at a cock fight?

A: He brings a duck.

Q: How do you know he's an Italian?

A: He bets on the duck.

Q: And how do you know the Mafia is at a cock fight?

A: The duck wins.

★ The last word on horses from John Tapp . . .

★ 'What's he doing shoeing a centipede?'

★ 'That gatekeeper wouldn't let the wind in without a ticket.'

★ 'They are bunched up like fleas on a dog's back.'

★ 'That horse wouldn't pull a skin off a custard.'

★ 'These binoculars are so strong I can see the jockeys changing their minds.'

★ 'What a thief! He'd steal the saddle off a nightmare.'

★ 'That horse can stay like a mother-in-law.'

Horizontal Chesterfield Rugby

★Marriage has many pains but celibacy has few pleasures.

—*Dr Samuel Johnson*

★ Here's to a game that's called ten toes—it's played all over town. The girls play it with ten toes up . . . the boys with ten toes down!

★ Girls, be careful of sports people. What starts off as a compliment often ends up with a confinement.

★ Norman and his very well-endowed wife were sitting in the stands before the big game. A guy walks up and says, 'Hello Norman, waiting for the game?' and then he fondles his wife's breast and moved on.

A few minutes later another guy comes up and says, 'Hello Norman, how are you doing?' gives his wife's breast a squeeze, and walks away.

This continues to happen for some time, to the amazement of the guy sitting next to Norman—who eventually turns to him and says, 'Listen pal, it's none of my business, but at least ten guys have come up and grabbed your wife's breast. What's going on?'

Norman looked at him very sadly and said, 'Well what can I do? If I leave her at home she sleeps with everybody!'

★ He arrives home and his wife greets him with news that the coach phoned and said that he's playing in the reserves this week.

'Oh, screw the coach,' he said angrily.

'I did, and you're back in the firsts next week.'

★ Golfers spend a lot of time away from home touring the world, and this can lead to marital problems. So the pro and his wife are seeing the marriage counsellor, who says, 'Now, you understand the repercussions of splitting up? Everything is halved—money, house, cars and jewellery?'

The pro says, 'What about our three children?'

The counsellor, seeing a chance to patch up the marriage, says, 'Well, obviously you cannot divide three children in half, so why don't you go back home, live together and have a fourth child, then you can take two and your wife can take two?'

The wife thought for a moment and then shook her head, 'No—that wouldn't work. If I had depended on him, I wouldn't have had the three kids I've got.'

★ If all the girls in the world were blades of grass, would all the boys be grasshoppers?

★ Marriage is a lot like a prize fight. Very often the preliminaries are better than the main event!

★ Beware of heat rash. Just because you are in love, don't promise anything rash.

★ They wouldn't let him take the stage name of Penis Van Lesbian, so he changed it to Dick Van Dyke.

★ It was going to be a sensational divorce. They both had reputations as swingers. She denied, however, that she had ever been promiscuous.

Eventually, on cross-examination, her husband's barrister said, 'I have one last question to ask you. Is it not true that on the morning of August the 11th, during a snow storm in the middle of Pitt Street, you had sex with a circus midget on the handlebars of a motorbike, that was driven by a trained monkey?'

The court lapsed into an astonished silence waiting for her laugh of denial.

She looked at the barrister straight in the eye and said, 'What was that date again?'

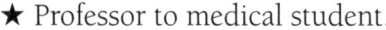

★ Professor to medical student.

'Miss O'Conner, what part of the human anatomy enlarges to ten times its normal size during periods of great excitement?'

She became so embarrassed she couldn't answer the question. However, the next student answered the question correctly when he said, 'The pupil of the eye.'

And the professor said, 'That's quite correct, and by the way, Miss O'Conner, your refusal to answer the question leads me to three conclusions:

1. You did not study last night's assignment.

2. You have a dirty mind.

3. Your honeymoon will be a tremendous disappointment.'

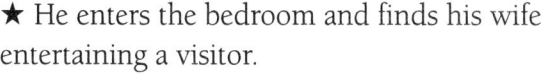

★ He enters the bedroom and finds his wife entertaining a visitor.

''ere, what's the game?' he asks.

And the visitor says, 'I don't know what it's called, but it will beat the hell out of basketball.'

★ I think there should be more sex education in this nation. How many times have you heard a girl say to you, 'What do you think you're doing?!'

★ She was so rough I wouldn't lay her with a brickie's trowel!

★ As Dorothy Parker once said, 'If all those sweet young things were laid end to end, I wouldn't be at all surprised.'

★ She combined her love life with tennis, which means she now serves in bed.

★ True love and a health body can make insomnia a pleasure.

★ Q: What's the difference between a dog and a fox?
A: About six drinks.

★ She was, it must be said, slightly promiscuous. In fact, she married Ken while she was engaged to Graham, so she could have a place to meet Bruce in order to make Ben jealous in front of Henry.

★ I once fell asleep with a cigarette in my hand and my wife lit it.

★ He is enamoured of the young lady who says to him, 'I cannot marry you, I'm a lesbian.'

And he said, 'That's all right—you go to your church and I'll go to mine!'

★ Then there was the unlucky young lover who went on a blind date and wound up at a disco with a guide dog.

★ They talk about young love and say, 'Matches are made in heaven.'

Well, if that is true, where do cigarette lighters come from?

★ Her husband was playing up, so she went to the priest.

'Father, help me. My husband takes no notice of me or the kids. Instead every night he's out drinking, carousing, chasing other women.'

The priest was very considerate. He said, 'I shall pray for you. Your husband is a miserable sinner.'

And the wife said, 'You are only half right, Father. A sinner he is, but miserable he's not. The bastard is having the time of his life.'

★ I'm at that wonderful age now—old enough to know better, but young enough to reconsider.

★ The wise man once said, 'Sex is the only game that becomes less exciting when played for money.'

★ All I need in a bachelor apartment is enough room to lay my head and a few close friends.

★ 'How much is your lawyer charging you for handling your divorce?'

'Oh, he's not charging me a penny,' said Dizzy Daphne. 'You see, he's a friend of my husband's: he's doing this as a favour to him.'

★ 'I honestly believe', said the wife, 'that you are ashamed to go out with me.'

'Don't be ridiculous dear, just wait until it is dark and I'll take you for a nice little walk.'

★ How do you tell which sperm is the happy one?
The one with egg on face!

★ The Irishman who thought Himalayas was a gay
chook and a Wank was an American with a harelip.

★ Q: Why do squirrels swim on their backs?
A: To keep their nuts dry!

★ Footballer on end-of-season trip. Love at first
sight on first night. After making mad passionate
love four times in quick succession, Miss World asks
for one more ride before she has to go home.

Footballer: 'That would be like trying to pot a snooker ball in the corner pocket using a piece of rope for a cue!'

Coaches and Minders

★There are two things you can be certain of: dying, and getting the arse as a football coach.

—*Royce Hart, Footscray coach 1980–82*

★ The coach is giving his usual boring motivational speech before the game and the players are paying no attention. He snaps at one of the players and says, 'Would you mind paying a little attention to what I'm saying?'

The player replied, 'I'm paying as little attention as I can.'

★ 'I am,' said the coach, 'the most honest man in sport. A lie has never passed my lips.'

'I suppose,' said one of the players, 'that's because all the time he talks through his arse.'

★ Of a certain coach it was once said, 'All he lacks is Hitler's moustache.'

★ The true definition of a sporting tragedy is to say that you will coach the club for nothing because you love that club, and then find out that they really have no money.

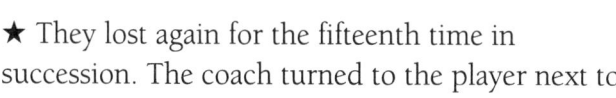

★ They lost again for the fifteenth time in succession. The coach turned to the player next to him and said, 'You're fired!'

The player said, 'Coach, I haven't played all season, I've been in the reserves.'

'I know,' said the coach. 'But if you can't get into this team you must be real bad.'

★ The ultimate insult to a losing football side is when the coach pokes his head around the dressing-room door and shouts, 'The team bus will be leaving in thirty minutes. Those who need showers take them.'

★ He once described his coach as 'Chaos in search of a frenzy'.

★ After the team's fourteenth straight defeat the press asked him for his comment.

He thought for a moment and said, 'Did you ever get the feeling that life is a black tuxedo and you are a pair of brown shoes?'

★ The departing coach looks at the new coach and says, 'You know, you are probably the second happiest man in the world.'

★ 'Welcome to our camp. This is your commander speaking. Today we are going to start our camp Olympics. Our first event is squash, and Colonel Clinger will be driving the steam-roller. This will be followed by cricket, where hut 12 will play hut 14 for the ashes of hut 13. Then the guards will practise at night for the shooting contest. Prisoners will help them by smoking cigarettes.'

★ You know the team is in trouble when the coach has a worried look on his assistant's face.

★ There is no such thing as job security for a football coach. As one coach said, 'All a lifetime contract means is I can't be fired during the first half if we are ahead and still in possession of the ball.'

★ The coach is giving them a pep talk. 'Right lads, here we are—unbeaten, untried and unscored against . . . and ready for our first game of the season.'

★ The coach said to the assembled players, 'I told you just last week, no sex before the game. Now, I know one of you disobeyed me and to show my disapproval I'm going to throw this chair at him.'

He picked up the chair and every player in the room ducked.

★ The local football coach had not won a game for ten years. Eventually he stood for Parliament, and in spite of his record, he got elected because in his policy speech he said that if he didn't get elected he'd have to go back to coaching.

★ Fans like to look up to football coaches.
    Either on a pedestal or a scaffold.

★ He was a good German coach. He collected all the jokes about himself and also the players who had made them.

★ A wonder coach . . . we sometimes wonder if he is a coach.

★ The losing coach was walking along the seafront when he saw a seagull hovering over head.

He looked up and said, 'Well, you may as well—everybody else does.'

★ He looked at the pair training and said, 'God, I wish I had five players like him.'

And the assistant coach said, 'Really?'

And the coach said, 'Yeah. I have ten like him. I wish I only had five.'

★ Coaching is the most precarious of all professions. Leading insurance companies now accept ten years in coaching as proof of permanent brain damage.

★ Asking that coach to give a motivational speech is like asking a deaf–mute to give a lecture on speech therapy.

★ One definition of a coach is: 'A man, who has to go through life being his own best friend'.

★ He was so obsessed with coaching, he actually came a bore.

People nowadays have parties just not to invite him.

★ A wise man once said, or then again maybe it was just a disgruntled player, 'There are two kinds of coaches: those who think they are God, and those who are sure of it.'

★ He has divided the club: 50 per cent don't want him to coach next year, and the other 50 per cent want him to resign right now.

★ The real reason coaches get angry is that they are in love with themselves but don't get on.

★ Coaches become paranoid when the results are not going their way. I know one, and every time the players huddled down for a scrum, he thought they were talking about him.

★ Don't you love it? The intellectual coach addressing the players after they've been beaten: 'I know you believe you understand what you think I said, but I'm not sure you realise what you heard is not what I meant to say.'

★ As a coach, his last wish was to be buried in his coffin face-down. Presumably so that the players could kiss him goodbye.

★ What a coach, what a coach. In twenty years he's been fired from every place except Cape Canaveral.

★ 'Why did you give up coaching?'

'Well, in my last club the coaching staff were afraid of the management, the management were afraid of the board of directors, the board of directors were afraid of the players, and when we played, the players were afraid of everyone.'

★ 'I am your new coach, my name is Eddie Edward. You man call me Mr Ed.'

'Well, that's unusual. We've never had a coach before who was a complete horse.'

★ He is lecturing his players.

'You are not just in sport, you are in the entertainment industry. You have to learn to cop criticism, being called vile names, receiving abusive phone calls. After all, one day, you may become a coach.'

★ A coach's job is so insecure that if half a dozen people knock on his door he wonders which one of them has the rope.

★ Then there was the female motor mechanic who disappeared and two weeks later she was found under a coach.

★ It was the club's annual talent quest and the reserve grade coach put his name down for a musical item.

He said, 'He would do what he had been doing all season—play second fiddle.'

★ Coaches are using video more and more as a coaching aid.

I know of one who, when asked if he enjoyed his honeymoon, said, 'I'll have to wait until I see the action replay.'

★ There are two kinds of coaches: those who have been fired and those who will be fired.

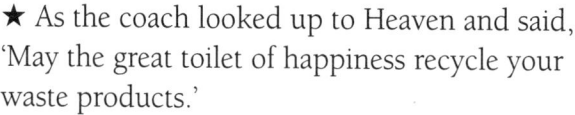

★ The coach is screaming at the player, 'I told you to kick on the fifth tackle. Can't you count?'

And the player said, 'Of course I can count: 1, 2, 3 and another and another.'

'Can't you count any higher than that?' the coach asked.

'Of course I can,' the player puts his hands over his head. '1, 2, 3, and other and other . . .'

★ As the coach looked up to Heaven and said, 'May the great toilet of happiness recycle your waste products.'

Young coach addresses the senior players—a hard bunch.

'I am going to be the boss here or know the reasons why . . .'

He's been there for two months and he now knows the reason why.

★ He was such an unpopular coach that the assistant coach's duties included food-tasting and starting his car.

★ What a player! He has more brains in his entire head than the rest of you have in your little fingers.

★ Does a coach's coach coach the coach according to his own coaching or does the coach doing the coaching coach the other coach according to the coach coach's coaching curriculum?

★ We call our coach 'Musket' because he's always loaded and gets fired every day.

★ He was a very dedicated coach as the sign on the door suggested: 'Closed because of death in the family—back in 20 minutes'.

★ In my experience I have found that a great coach is a crackpot who makes a screwball idea work.

★ Coach: 'Right lads, today we are going to practise passing the ball. Only this time it will be slightly different. We are going to try to pass it to our team mates.'

★ Before pre-season training even started, the coach told him to run 10 miles a day, and give him a ring at the end of the following week. After ten days he rang and the coach said, 'Why aren't you at training?'

And he said, 'I can't—I'm a hundred miles from here.'

★ 'You know, I do hope I die before my coach dies.'
'Why?'
'I want to get to Heaven before he has a chance to change it.'

★ Definition of a good coach: one who let's the club president beat him at golf.

★ 'Of course', said the chief executive, 'we should give the coach an increase in salary. It's much harder doing something when you know nothing about it.'

★ If he had half a brain he'd be a coach.
He has . . . and he is!

★ The beautiful Miss Australia was invited to lecture a group of coaches and she opened up with: 'The reason I am here today is that I have devised more defensive plays than the whole lot of you put together.'

★ Notice on club board: 'For Sale—complete set of sporting encyclopaedias. Never been used—Coach knows everything.'

★ When I look at his coaching career, I figure the only way he'll find contentment is to get amnesia.

★ At the annual general meeting of the Soccer Club, the continual interrupter was told by the chairman that he was out of order.

'Out of order?' said the heckler. 'How could I possible be out of order?'

'That', said the chairman, 'is a question that can only be answered by a vet.'

★ The rebel group was trying to oust the directors.

Their leader said, 'We represent the will of the supporters, 20,000 of whom have signed our petition anonymously.'

★ 'I have been the chairman of this club like my father and grandfather before me.'

A voice from the crowd said, 'Suppose your father and your grandfather were idiots—what would you be then?'

And he said, 'I'd be standing for treasurer.'

★ It had been a very tough annual general meeting and at last, the leader of the new group of directors got his chance to speak.

'The chairman', he said, 'has just given a speech which reminded me of a Texas Longhorn—a point here, a point there, and a lot of bull in between.

'His speech was also like a river, narrow at the head, broad at the mouth and completely wet throughout. Or perhaps it was like a boat—he tooted loudest but in a fog.

'The boat that most closely resembles his speech, however, is Noah's Ark—for his speech drifted endlessly on the waters and was filled with a kind of strange things.

'In biblical days it was considered a miracle if an ass spoke, but after listening to that speech I realise that times have changed.'

★ The story that would have been true of so many clubs in days gone by. The chairman calls the young player into his office.

'Listen, young man,' he says. 'This is your first season with the club, and I gather that there is a bit of jealousy with some of the more senior players. But I am going to take a chance with you. Not only are you in the first team this week, but you are going to be the captain. Now what do you think of that?'

The young man said, 'I am overwhelmed. It really is very nice of you, dad.'

SPORTS JOKES

★ 'Right, lads,' said the chairman of selectors. 'All those in favour say "aye" and those against say "I resign"'.

★ It was first said about Winston Churchill, but it can be equally said about a lot of club chairmen: 'There but for the grace of God goes God.

★ Officials of football clubs should always remember that they are appointed, and not anointed.

★ The sports agent is pitching to the head of the movie studio.

'I have this dog, his name is Rocky. He talks, he runs the mile, he skips with a rope.'

And the studio head says, 'What kind of dog is he?'

'He's a boxer.'

And the studio head says, 'Nah, a boxer named Rocky? It's been done.'

★ Then there was the sports agent who was so good with numbers, he eventually got to wear one for ten to fifteen years.

★ As a sports promoter he was very difficult to get to do business with. His office hours were only 2 to 4 and that was just on visiting days.

★ I once knew a sports agent who fell into the shark-infested pool and escaped unharmed.

As I've always said, 'Sharks will never touch one of their own.'

Later when it was found out that he had thrown himself into the shark-infested waters, he was prosecuted by the RSPCA.

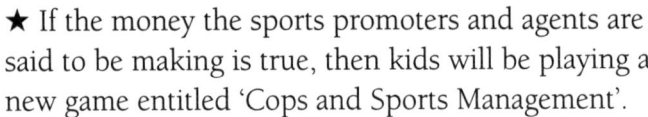

★ If the money the sports promoters and agents are said to be making is true, then kids will be playing a new game entitled 'Cops and Sports Management'.

★ Then the sports agent phoned the proprietor of the exclusive men's shop, and said, 'I've just found out that the player I manage owes you for a suit.'

'That's true', said the owner. 'Have you come to

settle the account?'

'No,' said the agent.

'I'd just like a suit on the same terms.'

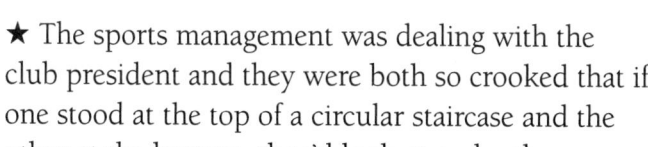

★ The sports management was dealing with the club president and they were both so crooked that if one stood at the top of a circular staircase and the other at the bottom, they'd look at each other straight in the eye.

★ The basketball coach of a big college team was trying to explain away a particularly disappointing defeat.

'The whole team played like a bunch of amateurs,' he confessed.

★ It is said about a certain sports journalist that he has such a high regard for truth, he reserves it for special occasions.

★ He was that sort of a sports interviewer: every time you agree with him, he changes his mind. He asks you a question, answers it for you and then says you're wrong.

★ There are over 100,000 words in the English Language that are seldom used, and if it wasn't for Rex Mossop we wouldn't even know what they were.

★ No matter what the newspapers said about him he never worried—he always said, 'Words will never hurt me.'

He died yesterday when a neon sign fell on his head.

★ The agent said to the club president, 'I want the same conditions as my boy had with the last club, plus a 25 per cent increase in salary.'

'What conditions were those?' asked the president.

'Well, hospital benefits, life insurance, free car, phone bill, rent paid, overseas trips, Christmas bonuses, kids' education paid.'

The president asked, 'But why would you leave a club like that?'

And the agent said, 'They went bankrupt.'

★ He was a hard, tough negotiator, and he just got the best deal in the world for his clients. As he left, he turned to the chief executive and said, 'I know you wish I was dead, so that you could dance on my grave.'

'Not me,' said the angry chief executive. 'When I left the army I swore I'd never join another queue.'

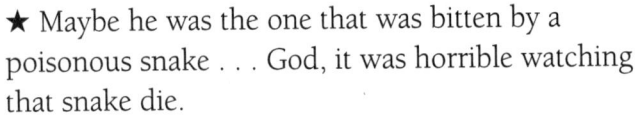

★ Maybe he was the one that was bitten by a poisonous snake . . . God, it was horrible watching that snake die.

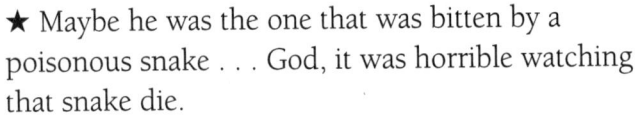

★ Two agents were each trying to sell their client to the club for the coaching position.

The president looked at them both and said, 'Let's face it, neither of your guys can coach much. They are both desperate for a job. I honestly believe both of them would sell their mothers to get this job.'

'You are right', said one agent, 'but at least my man would deliver.'

★ Well, I know my manager—he has a great head for money. It's got a little slot on the top.

★ Mick Stone, the ARL umpires' boss was touring small country towns giving lectures on the rules.

'Now, what would happen,' he said, 'if at the last kick of the game, the ball burst in mid-air, with half the ball going over the bar and half going under?'

The old committee man thought for a moment and said, 'Well . . . the way I see it, the club would be down about $60.'

★ He really knows where a dollar is to be found. Thomas Edison may have discovered electricity, but my guy was the one who discovered the meter.

★ 'What do you think of him as an umpire?'

'This is the third game I've seen him umpire, and I must admit my opinion of him has risen to almost zero.'

★ A funny statistic: umpires only account for 0.001 per cent of the population, but 40 per cent of the nation's abuse.

★ The difference between an umpire and a trampoline is that you have to take your boots off before you jump on the trampoline.

★ The only good thing you can say about that umpire is that his brother is worse.

★ The police quite often have to escort the umpire from the ground. This presents no problem for the police because they are used to helping the blind.

★ 'Hey umpire, is it true you once walked into a pet shop and ordered a hot dog?'

★ 'That umpire is a bastard.'

'No, I know for a fact that the umpire is not a bastard.'

'Well, who's his father?'

'Anonymous donor 127.'

★ Nobody likes umpires better than I do, and I hate them.

★ 'Hey umpire, if brains were made out of skunks you wouldn't have a smell.'

★ 'If brainstorms were cyclones you wouldn't whip up enough to ruffle the wings of a butterfly.'

★ 'Hey umpire! If it rains you won't need an umbrella. A horse's tail will cover what you really are.'

★ 'Hey umpire! If you were nude you would still be a disgrace to the uniform.'

★ 'Hey umpire! Your wife must like the simple things in life. She married one.'

★ 'Hey umpire! Do you know why I am fascinated by your brain? I collect miniatures.'

★ 'Hey umpire! Do you know why you will never have piles? It's because you are already a perfect arse.'

★ 'Hey umpire! If you had a brain tumour the first thing the doctor would do is look up your arse.'

★ 'Hey umpire! What happened? Did your rocking horse kick you in the head?'

★ 'Hey umpire! If bad decision's were a laxative you'd need a ten-tonne toilet.'

★ 'Hey umpire! This game needs you like a mermaid needs a gynaecologist.'

★ 'Hey umpire! Why don't we form a suicide pact? You go first.'

★ 'Hey umpire! If stupidity was music, you'd be a brass band.'

★ 'Hey umpire! Do you know the difference between an umpire and a white line? Well, the law says that you mustn't run over a white line.'

★ 'Hey umpire! Isn't it sad that birth control can't be radioactive?

★ 'Hey umpire! If they put a brick on your head they could call it an extension.'

★ The umpire was wearing glasses over his contact lenses.

★ I once followed an umpire at confession. I had to wait three and a half hours.

★ 'Hey umpire! Why don't you introduce your mind to your mouth?'

★ 'Hey umpire! Why don't you introduce your whistle to your mouth?'

★ I'll tell you about that umpire—he's brighter than he looks, but then again, he'd have to be.

★ A voice from the crowd was shouting 'Kill the umpire, kill the umpire'. It was his wife.

★ They call him candlelight because he doesn't get any brighter.

★ 'Hey umpire! If your head was a petrol tank the needle would be on empty.'

★ 'Hey umpire! Is it true that your brother was an only child?'

★ 'Hey umpire! Do you realise that you are the living proof that you are never too old to learn a new way of doing something stupid?'

★ 'Let me tell you, we need you like a rooster needs a marriage licence.'

★ 'Hey umpire! I don't know what your wattage is, but you're no chandelier.'

★ 'Hey umpire! I'm not saying you're a cheat, but if you ever told the truth it would have stretch marks.'

★ 'Hey umpire! Do you know what you problem is? When your mother used to rock you to sleep she didn't use a big enough rock.'

★ 'Hey umpire! If you want to put a gleam in your eye, shine a flashlight in one of your eyes.'

★ 'Hey umpire! Do the rest of the Muppets know you're here?'

★ 'Hey umpire! If brains were dynamite, you wouldn't have enough to blow your nose.'

★ 'Hey umpire! If you were a building you'd be condemned.'

★ 'Hey umpire! If they ever brainwash you, they'll use a tumble for a bucket.'

★ 'Umpire—is it true your mother bought a do-it-yourself kit for an idiot?'

★ The gods gave man flame and he invented bushfire.

They gave him love and he invented marriage.

They gave him football and he invented umpires.

★ Referee to egotistical player: 'How did you start?'

'Well, in the beginning, I created the heavens and the Earth.'

★ She said to her friend: 'My husband speaks three languages—golf, cricket and football.'

★ Doctor: Should I give him a local anaesthetic?'

Manager: 'No, he's our star player, give him the best—something imported.'

★ The only way to win an argument with an umpire is to be on his side.

★ He had been studying at the Australian Institute of Sport for three years longer than any other student. Eventually he was called to the Dean's office.

'Smith,' the Dean said, 'you have been here longer than anyone else and your grades show you have the lowest coordination of anyone who has attended the Institute.

'You have a complete lack of skills and a total absence of knowledge about the game.

'It is our recommendation that you consider becoming a coach.'

★ I wouldn't say he has an ego, but he is absolutely convinced that if he hadn't been born, people would want to know why not.

★ The club nutritionist is on a health food kick—whatever he gets his hand on he puts in the blender.

Last week I drank a chicken.

★ This has nothing to do with sport, but I once saw a sign at an anti-nuclear demonstration that said, 'Make love, not war'.

I thought . . . I'm married I do both . . . then again, maybe it does have something to do with sport.

★ Heard at training: 'Hey, you dropped those weights on my foot.'

'Well, why don't you put your foot where it belongs?'

'Don't tempt me.'

★ He found the magic bottle and rubbed it. When the genie appeared he said, 'I want to be able to play golf like Norman, cricket like Bradman, fight like Ali and have money like Kerry Packer.'

And the genie said, 'Listen, you idiot, if I had a set-up like that do you think I'd be living in this crummy bottle?'

★ He was a 'Norm': the ultimate armchair sportsman. In fact, when you opened his refrigerator a little the television set goes on.

★ Doctors tell you that if you eat slowly, you will eat less. This is very true, especially if you are at the team's BBQ, or you happen to be the member of a large family.

★ When asked the difference between a crowd and a congregation, the sporting vicar replied 'A crowd listens. A congregation doesn't.'

Boxing and Wrestling

★When I get through with the bum he'll be all covered in blood—my blood.

—Jimmy Durante

★ I love it when the journalists write 'It was a great conflict'.

A real conflict is when one man wants to be a boxer and the other a violinist, and they're Siamese twins.

★ There are winners and there are losers. I don't want to say he's a loser, but they once threw him out of the library for being too quiet.

★ First burglar cried out, 'Let's get out of here. I've just realised we've broken into Jeff Fenech's house.'

Second burglar said, 'Don't let it bother you. I know for a fact that he won't fight for anything less than a quarter of a million.'

★ What that man knows about boxing would fill a hospital.

★ He was famous for his three-legged punch. He used to hit them with his stool.

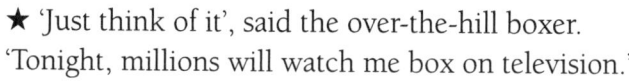

★ 'Just think of it', said the over-the-hill boxer. 'Tonight, millions will watch me box on television.'

'Yes,' said the manager, 'and they'll know the result at least ten seconds before you do.'

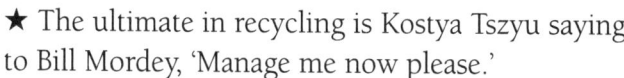

★ The ultimate in recycling is Kostya Tszyu saying to Bill Mordey, 'Manage me now please.'

★ He was taking a terrible beating, and as he stumbled back to his corner and sat on his stool, his manager looked at him and said, 'Let him hit you with his left hand—your face is becoming lop-sided.'

★ I won't say he's had one fight too many, but he's the only man I know who has reached his second childhood for the third time.

★ 'I once fought Mike Tyson.'
  'Oh, how long did you last?'
  'Exactly four Hail Marys.'

★ The question is: if Don King was knocked down by a bus who would be elected head of boxing?

The answer is, of course, the bus driver.

★ He is taking a terrible beating. At the end of round 3, his corner man says, 'You're doing great, he hasn't laid a glove on you.'

He looks at him through his half-closed eyes and says, 'Well, watch the umpire. There is some bastard out there beating the crap out of me.'

★ He was knocked out in the first round but accepted his defeat graciously, congratulated his opponent, shook hands with the umpire, left the ring and shot his manager and trainer.

★ He was the cream of the boxing stable, which is possibly why at every fight, he got whipped.

★ Don King is the most powerful man in boxing. When he stands up Toyotas jump in the air.

★ At the press conference the manager's promoting his fighter.

'My boy,' he said, 'pound for pound is probably the best boxer in the world.'

One of the journalists said, 'That's a joke. I've seen him fight and he couldn't hurt a fly.'

And quick as a flash, the manager said, 'I'll prove you wrong, produce the fly.'

★ Boxing contracts have always had a clause about who to notify in the case of an accident.

Some answer wife, parent, brother. The cleverest one writes down 'How about a good doctor?'

★ There is always a nice way of saying things. As the boxer said, 'He didn't just beat me—he knocked me inconstipated.'

★ Let me tell you how much of an animal that boxer is . . . we traced his family tree back to the garden of Eden, and he's not related to either Adam or Eve.

★ It was once said of a boxer, who had had one fight too many, he could jump out of a plane and not know if he was going up or down.

★ Have you noticed how much weight heavyweight boxers put on when they retire and stop training? It's like watching the birth of a mountain.

★ You know they're overweight when that cute little dimple on their knee is their belly button.

★ Boxers are great believers in democracy. They always look out for the rights of others.

★ Joe Bugner, who has had more retirements to his credit than his superannuation fund, is quite a man.

As he says himself, 'Age is an attitude. I am retreaded, not retired.'

★ The rabbi and the priest sat together ring-side.

When one of the boxers knelt in his corner and blessed himself, the rabbi said, 'Does that really help?'

And the priest said, 'Of course it does, but only if he can punch.'

'Well, what would happen', said the rabbi, 'if both of them blessed themselves?'

'Well', the priest smiled, 'God would look down and say "This is going to be one Hell of a fight".'

★ You have a fair idea a fight is fixed when one of the fighters enters the ring carrying a can of beer and an airline ticket.

★ As a boxer he had a lazy life, he never got up before 10.

★ 'I don't want to box for the army again. You can't make me box for the army.'

'You're quite right', said the colonel, 'but we can put the gloves on you, put you in the centre of the ring with your opponent, ring the bell, and from then on, you can use your own judgement.'

★ He was knocked out in the first round, and they had to help him to the canvas.

★ He was not much of a boxer. In fact, in his first six fights he never got to use his stool.

He was taking a terrible hiding in the ring. 'Last round coming up', he says to his second. 'How am I doing?'

'Well', said the second, 'if you knock him out, you may get a draw.'

★ He'd had one fight too many.

He said, 'I want one last fight. I want to fight Killer McQueen. I can outbox him, I can outfight him. You have to get me a fight with Killer McQueen.'

His manager said, 'If I've told you once, I've told you a thousand times: you are Killer McQueen.'

★ After Lionel Rose knocked out Rocky Guthrie, he was taken to see a movie of the fight.

His only comment was, 'It had a happy ending.'

★ He took a dive but the umpire knew it and kept counting: 11, 12, 13.

When he got to 110 the fighter opened one eye and said, 'Mister Umpire, you is very kind, but I'm through for the night.'

★ I'm managing a crossword fighter.

He enters the ring vertical and leaves it horizontal.

★ Heavyweight boxing contenders are now becoming older and bigger.

For his training George Foreman runs three laps around the track. Joe Bugner goes one better. He runs three laps around George Foreman.

★ He had fought 22 fights, winning them all.

They brought over a very tough middleweight. A flurry of blows, and our local and very intelligent fighter is dropped in the first round.

During the fight postmortem they asked, 'Did he hurt you?'

Our very intelligent fighter said, 'No, but he was going to.'

★ He had had one fight too many and he told the doctor that he was not a boxer any more. He was a cocker spaniel.

'How long have you been a cocker spaniel?' was the doctor's reply.

'Well Doc, not that long. I used to be a St Bernard but I lost my liquor licence.'

★ There have been some very bad decisions in boxing, but none worse than the day Murphy fought Kowalski, with Casey as the umpire.

Murphy is taking a terrible beating, down for the third time. Casey stands over him, 'One. What are you doing, lying there you idiot! You're fighting for the honour of Ireland.

'Two. Didn't I tell you to get up? Your father is watching, your brother is watching, the whole of Ireland is watching.

'Three—this is the longest count in history.'

Murphy staggers to his feet, Kowalski rushes in for the kill, but he slips on the canvas.

Casey is in there in a flash, 'One . . . two . . . two fives are ten, you're finished. Murphy wins by a knockout.'

★ 'How did you let him beat you? He was nearly a foot shorter—God, man he only came up to your chin.'

'I know, but he came up an awful lot.'

★ Funny world: the other night I went to the fights and a soccer match erupted.

★ What about the Irishman who thought Sugar Diabetes was a Spanish boxing champion?

★ They actually have a hotel in Darwin that has nude baked bean wrestling. I must admit it's very entertaining, but the sandwiches taste pretty ordinary afterwards.

★ Just before his World Championship wrestling match the trainer had given Pat the last piece of advice: 'Don't let him get you in his coconut hold. If he does, you're a goner . . . nobody has ever got out of the mad Russian's coconut hold.'

Two minutes into the first round the Russian has Paddy in his coconut hold. Paddy's trainer puts his hands in his face and says, 'I don't want to look, I don't want to look.'

Then there's an enormous cheer, the crowd goes berserk. Paddy has broken the coconut hold . . . for the first time in the world, the coconut hold has been broken and he's pinned the mad Russian to the canvas.

Back in his corner the trainer hugs him and says, 'I can't believe it! Nobody has ever done it before. How on Earth did you break the mad Russian's coconut hold?'

'Well', says Paddy, 'he got my body twisted in that coconut. I never felt so much pain in my entire life. I thought I was going to pass out. And then I saw two testicles hanging down in front of my eyes, and with one last effort, I bit those two testicles. It's amazing what a man can do when he bites his own testicles.'

★ Professional wrestling is a very hard sport, particularly if you haven't taken acting lessons.

★ I know one wrestler who tried to push start a submarine.

★ First wrestler: 'Did you know the doctors have proved that when we wrestle we only use one third of our brain?'

Second wrestler: 'That's absolutely ridiculous, what happens to the other one third?'

★ The biggest educational problem in wrestling is kindergarten drop-out.

★ The referee had finished talking to the two wrestlers in the centre of the ring and said, 'Now, those are the rules. Now go back to your corner and come out acting.'

★ Back to wrestling: if we weren't descended from apes, explain how we've got professional wrestlers.

★ He always wanted to be the star attraction at the Entertainment Centre. Unfortunately he went on the wrong night and Jeff Fenech knocked him out in the fourth round.

Large Balls and Small

★It is harder to be a good winner than a good loser— one has less practice.

★ At a very exclusive tennis club they even have a full-time gardener on staff. Every morning he arrives to water the lawn, the flowers and the liquor.

★ The computer could answer any question and the conceited tennis coach asked, 'How many great tennis coaches have there been?'

Out came the answer, 'One less than you think.'

★ There is nothing boring about winning. In my whole life I've never heard anyone say, 'Oh dammit I've won again.'

★ I wasn't a good tennis player. The only time I came to the net was to congratulate the winner.

★ Q: What do you call a girl standing in the middle of the tennis court?

A: Annette.

★ Martina Navratilova has retired from tennis. She is now appearing on Broadway in her own one-man show.

★ Newsreader: 'In an unusual incident today, a tennis umpire was fired for swearing at John McEnroe.'

★ Funny thing about John McEnroe, even though he had a great backhand he was more famous for his one-finger forehand.

★ I hate it when the losers congratulate the winners: they have as much sincerity as a lifetime guarantee with a three-month warranty!

★ Speaking to her friend she said, 'That was the most boring tennis dance I've ever been to.'

'Well,' said her friend, 'if it was so boring why did you stay all night?'

'Well, I had to. I couldn't find my clothes.'

★ They just finished two sets of tennis, and as they were walking off the court, she said, 'I've been taking tennis lessons. So far it's cost me nearly $10,000.'

'Oh', said her partner, 'you should call my brother.'

'Oh, is he a pro?'

'No, he's a lawyer. He'll help you get your money back.'

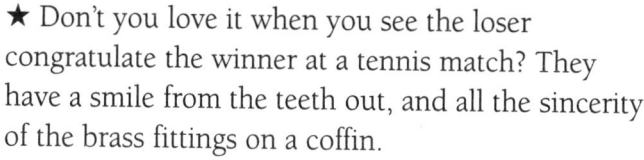

★ Don't you love it when you see the loser congratulate the winner at a tennis match? They have a smile from the teeth out, and all the sincerity of the brass fittings on a coffin.

★ At the veterans' tennis tournament both players' teeth fell out.

The score was one set all.

★ The sincerity of two female tennis players kissing each other after a final can only be compared to boxers shaking hands before a fight.

★ The new John McEnroe tennis racquet—when you lose it, it flies off the handle.

★ The coloured player said to three white players, 'Anyone for mixed doubles?'

★ He bet his boss that Sampras would beat Agistini, and sure enough, Sampras did it in three sets. So he collected the $100 in cash and said to his boss, 'Do you know what I'm going to do? I'm going to frame this $100 note and hang it over my bar, just to show that I'm smarter than my boss.'

'In that case', said the boss, 'why don't you give me back the cash and I'll give you a cheque?'

★ Tennis is the only social occasion where you pray for bad service.

★ At the annual trophy presentation, the boring president began his speech 'I only have ten minutes and I honestly don't know where to start.'

Voice from the back yelled 'How about at the ninth!'

★ Tennis is like claiming alimony; 'love' means nothing.

★ As the tom cat said while watching the Wimbledon finals: 'I've got a brother in that racquet.'

★ I first got suspicious that he was on drugs when the ball hit the white line and he bent down and started to sniff it.

★ I'm getting into much better shape for tennis. It's now taking me two sets before I turn purple.

★ 'Why don't you play tennis with Jim any more?'

'Would you play tennis with someone who doesn't call lines and cheats all the time?'

'No, of course not.'

'Well, neither will Jim.'

★ When my opponent hits the ball to me, my brain immediately barks out a command to my body: 'Race up to the net,' it says. 'Slam the ball to the right-hand far corner, jump back into position to return the next volley.'

'What then?' asked his friend.

Then my body says, 'Who, me?'

★ The more I watch basketball the more I like small people.

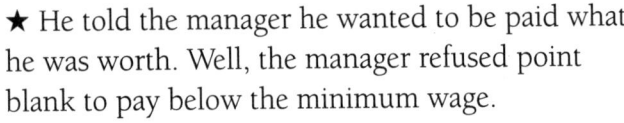

★ He told the manager he wanted to be paid what he was worth. Well, the manager refused point blank to pay below the minimum wage.

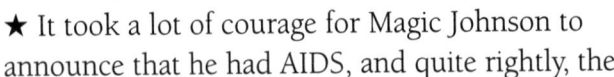

★ When I watch some of these very tall basketball players, I often wonder if they had to wear their brothers' hand-me-ups when they were kids.

★ It took a lot of courage for Magic Johnson to announce that he had AIDS, and quite rightly, the press applauded his courage. Then, as he was leaving the press conference, he blew them a kiss and everybody ducked.

★ Today in Adelaide the $20 million basketball and multi sports centre which was designed and approved by the defence department to withstand an all out nuclear attack, was totally wrecked by teenagers.

★ He was not the sharpest knife in the draw, but he was a genius with a basketball. In fact, he could do anything with a basketball except autograph it.

★ The owner of the club was speaking to the members.

He said, 'Listen—before we elect a coach, we need to know if he can stand up to the incredible stress generated by the job of everyday basketball. That is why I'm recommending that all future coaches serve two full years as a school bus driver.'

★ I love watching American basketball. Where else can you go and abuse millionaires?

★ First bowler says, 'I suppose we shouldn't be playing bowls on a Sunday. We should have gone to church.'

Second bowler replies, 'I couldn't have gone to church today, my wife is very sick.'

★ He was a baseball fanatic all his life, and a very excitable one.

Eventually he bought a race horse for recreation. First race, two yards from the winning post, his horse is involved in what is certainly going to be a triple photo finish.

He can contain himself no longer . . . his baseball training takes over and at the top of his voice he yells, 'Slide, you bastard.'

★ A barber named Cohan became a bowling fanatic. One day, in the middle of a great game, his superior rings him at the alley, telling him to come back to the shop as he needs a shave.

To which Cohan replied, 'No way—a bowling Cohan lathers no boss.'

★ She was only a female baseball player, but she wouldn't play ball without a diamond.

★ The Mafia had a ten-pin bowling tournament, where first prize was a cheque for $40,000 or $100 in cash. Second prize was a car; the exact colour and model to be determined sometime later that night.

★ The first woman enthused, 'I'm so excited! Last night I came as close as I have ever come to bowling a perfect three hundred.'

Second lady said, 'That's wonderful, what did you bowl?'

She said, 'Sixty-six.'

★ 'I'm never home, I'd rather play bowls, ten-pin bowling. than eat.'

'Oh, doesn't your wife object?'

'No, she'd rather play bingo than cook.'

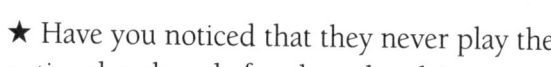

★ Have you noticed that they never play the national anthem before lawn bowls?

Possibly they're afraid that some of the players may not be able to stand up.

★ Best bit of sporting advice ever received: if you're bald and have a hole in your head, never go ten-pin bowling.

★ Be kind to animals: kiss an ice hockey player.

★ The bible says you should love your enemies, bless those who curse you, and pray for those who do you harm. What this means is that no Christian should play ice hockey.

★ Ice hockey is a sport where mostly the puck gets in the way of a good game.

★ Ice hockey is one of those sports you hope your enemies play.

★ Ice hockey must be one of the toughest games in the world. I always get the feeling when I watch it that if some of those guys entered the human race they'd be disqualified.

★ Ice hockey is the most violent of sports. I know a player who, last year, on the way home from the Stanley Cup game, was mugged three times and didn't realise it.

★ Smallest book in the world: *Ice Hockey players who are members of Mensa.*

★ He actually took up lion taming for a living. He used to be an ice hockey player, but lost his nerve.

★ How do you recognise an ice hockey player in a string quartet?

Well, he's the one putting down his trumpet.

★ Ice hockey is very tough and can be very dangerous. Most players go for a few pints after the game.

So, never play ice hockey if you belong to a rare blood group.

★ Three girls in the netball team were in the café, crying their eyes out. The local parish priest walked over and said, 'Please girls, don't cry. We'll order some tea and you can tell me your problems.'

Well, the pot of tea arrived and the priest looked around for somebody to pour it, 'Now, who's going to be mother?'

And the three netball players cried louder than ever.

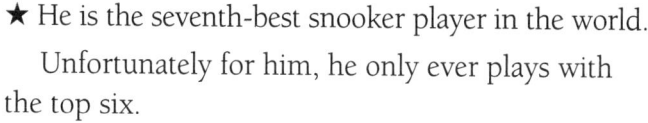

★ He is the seventh-best snooker player in the world.

Unfortunately for him, he only ever plays with the top six.

★ He had a terrible death—he swallowed a complete set of billiard balls and snookered himself.

★ Two players from Mentalsville played snooker all night and didn't pot a ball.

'Next time,' said one of them, 'I think we'll take the wooden triangle from around the balls.'

★ 'Doctor, I am not well.'

'Well, maybe it's your diet, what are you eating?'

'Snooker balls.'

'You're kidding me—just snooker balls?'

'Yes, this morning I had two reds and a blue. Lunch I'll have another two reds, a pink and a yellow.'

'And what will you have for dinner?'

'Four reds, a white and a black.'

'Well, that's your problem. You're not getting enough greens.'

★ 'Doctor, Doctor, I feel like a snooker ball.'

Doctor: 'Get to the end of the cue.'

★ Eddie Charlton, that great snooker champion is in the middle of nowhere, so he goes into the RSL club, and there is a guy on his own at the snooker table.

He doesn't recognise Eddie and says, 'Do you fancy a game?'

Charlton answers, 'I don't mind.' Being a pro from way back, he says, 'What will you give me for a start?'

The bloke says, 'I couldn't give you a start—I've never seen you play.'

Charlton's break hits the top red into the middle pocket—not an easy shot. Then a black, a red, a black, a red, a black for every red. Straight through the colours—yellow, green, brown, blue, pink and black . . . cleans the table.

Maximum break 147.

The local looks in astonishment and Charlton says, 'Fancy another game?'

He says, 'I don't mind, but what will you give me for a start?'

Charlton says, 'I couldn't give you a start—I've never seen you play.'

★ Polo is hockey with fertiliser.

Hunting and Fishing

★Scholars have long known that fishing eventually turns men into philosophers. Unfortunately it is almost impossible to buy decent tackle on a philosopher's salary.

—Pat F. McManus

★ 'How many fish have you caught?'

'Well, if I catch the one I'm after and two more, I'll have three.'

★ Glass-bottomed boats are a good idea. It means the fish can see how big the guy they got away from is.

★ The 55 kg breaking strain nylon fishing line snapped as the tiny loop around the small metal bollard fastened tightly. Whatever had momentarily taken the bait on the end of my rapidly diminishing handline, treated the fine, almost invisible thread, like a piece of cotton!

It was difficult for a relatively non sea-loving person like myself to gauge the power and dimensions of the creature lurking beneath the sparkling blue-green tropical waters. Not to mention the potential danger!

The action of my leather-gloved companion in yanking against the drag of the tackle, then gaining sufficient slack to loop it around the chrome-plated fixture on the boat's handrail, certainly saved me from getting wet, maybe even losing the bottom half of my right leg. True to form, I had tangled most of the line in a huge mess beneath my feet. No wonder my nickname's Tanglefoot!

This little saga had begun by pulling in what I thought was about 3 or 4 kilos of fish, but some monster of a fish had other ideas and must have followed my catch on its painful journey to the surface.

Then, without warning, my hand-line whistled through my helpless fingers at a frantic pace, back into the depths below. The fine nylon cord cut like a knife through the index finger of my right hand. Blood streamed freely from the widening wound . . . a burning sensation followed and I immediately let go of the line.

My bare feet thrashed up and down like a piston in an attempt to keep clear of the snaking fishing line as it disappeared over the edge.

Directions were being shouted at me from everyone, but too late. I was desperately in trouble with my footwork—the pale green fishing line was pulling taut against my right leg, just above the ankle . . . three or more coils tightened. Blood started to dribble slowly down my leg . . .

Even worse was that I was being dragged overboard . . . by the leg! Yes, the huge fish, or whatever, was winning this tug of war, and I couldn't get my hand near the razor sharp line!

My host, Gary, realised the seriousness of my predicament before my head crashed against the aluminium bottom of the twin-hulled shark cat.

His experience quickly showed as he grabbed my line, and as they say . . . the rest is history. A classic case of the one that got away. He would have been a beauty! But . . . just as well that line snapped, eh?

★ I'll tell you how big the fish was that got away: I was using a whale as bait.

The fish was so big it took two men to carry the photograph.

★ All this happened after I'd completed reading the script for a new television commercial . . . yours truly was cast in the role, unfairly, as the world's worst fisherman.

Who do you think my partner in the dinghy was to be? My mate and former cricketing great Dougie Walters. We were both happy to be drinking the product—Tooheys 2.2 light beer.

The shoot turned out to be very funny for all involved except Dougie. Our dinghy was the most unstable vessel I have ever been asked to go fishing in—1.5 metres of round-bottomed aluminium with two baby oars.

The concept was for both 'heroes' to end up overboard after successfully delivering our scripted lines. But nobody had mentioned this to Doug. In all we had seven identical pairs of shorts and T-shirts, in case we didn't get our words right first up. Yes, we were going to get very wet and more than once . . . just so the cameraman could get his act together. The other fact that Dashing Doug failed to mention was that he couldn't swim . . . minor detail but important when you're 50 metres from shore.

Well, sure enough, the first time I rock the boat and upend Doug in the process . . . I knee him on the back of the head as we fall into the sea.

Now what would you do if one of the great practical jokers of the world asks for help . . . you just let him sink back under for a second dip.

As he surfaced again . . . looking and sounding in real distress I must admit I thought twice . . . The cries became more frantic but I still thought he was having a lend of me. So under the water went his head again.

Finally, as he surfaced for the *third* time I could see he'd swallowed copious quantities of sea water and was in real trouble.

This is where my *Herald* Learn to Swim Certificate came in handy. I cupped my hand under his chin and instructed him not to struggle or I'd knock him out completely.

Slowly but surely the pair of us progressed towards the beach to the waiting gathering of anxious onlookers.

There were two options. One was to press on his ribcage then extend his arms to work his lungs. The other was not a nice alternative . . . mouth-to-mouth resuscitation with a bloke who smokes eighty cigarettes, on a good day.

I whispered in Doug's ear that I thought the world of him but not enough to suck lips with him, so pressure on the ribs it was.

Most importantly, I had to drag his bum out of the water as I stretched the water-logged Aussie legend onto the wet sand . . . because had it remained even in two or three inches I would have siphoned half the ocean . . . in one end and out the other.

As it was he coughed up plenty . . . and I doubt if he'd ever felt that crook even after a long innings on the Tooheys.

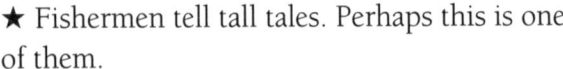

★ He's telling his story over a beer, 'Let me tell you now, plenty of fishermen have hooked that fish. But I was the one that caught him, not that it did me much good, because we couldn't eat him.'

'Why ever not?'

'Well, he had so many fish hooks in him, I got more money by selling him for scrap metal.'

★ Fishermen tell tall tales. Perhaps this is one of them.

'I kid you not—the fish were that big . . . Every time I caught one of them the lake's water level went down. When I finished, I'd caught that many fish the boat was practically on a dry bed . . . I had to throw six fish back so as the boat would float.'

★ He took his own scales whenever he went in for a fishing competition, and weighed every fish he ever caught in front of the other fishermen.

One day one of the other fishermen's wife gave birth unexpectedly. The midwife borrowed his scales and—lo and behold—the baby weighed 17 kg.

★ Early in the morning he opens the door to find the police sergeant outside.

The sergeant says, 'Does Mrs Halpin live here?'

He said, 'Yes, She's my mother-in-law.'

'Well, I'm sorry to inform you, sir, but we found her floating in the water this morning with ten lobsters attached to her.'

'Oh dear!'

'What would you like us to do with her?'

'Well, you take five lobsters, I'll take five lobsters and we'll set her again tomorrow.'

★ Ice-fishing was his sport. He once brought home a hundred pounds of ice. His wife drowned trying to cook it.

★ There is no logic to fishing. You sit all day waiting to catch a fish, and then you go home and complain if your wife has dinner ten minutes late.

★ If you catch a fresh salmon, the best part to eat is the tail end, starting from just behind the ear.

★ They were trying to impress each other with their fishing exploits.

The first guy said, 'I once had a four-hour fight with a 300-pound salmon, biggest fish I've ever caught.'

Second guy said, 'Well, I've never caught anything like that, but I once snagged a lantern from the bottom of the lake and the lantern had a tag on it proving it was lost back in 1897. The amazing thing is, it was a waterproof lantern, and the light was still on.'

Well, the first fisherman was silent for a few minutes and with a thoughtful look on his face, said slowly, 'I'll tell you what I'll do—I'll take 100 pounds off my salmon if you put out the light in your lantern.'

★ 'Yesterday I went fishing with my wife.'

'Oh, did you catch anything?'

'No, not a thing. I think I'll go back to using worms.'

★ It was his wife's birthday, so he bought her a beautiful fishing rod.

'She must have been pleased with that?'

'Not really, she was expecting a car.'

★ Life can be unjust.

He caught a 70-pound fish in the first round of the competition, but couldn't carry on because he had dislocated both shoulders describing it.

★ The river is very good for fish. I can't get any of them to leave it.

★ It is said that the reason most women don't go fishing is that they have more important things to lie about.

★ I love it when he says, 'I'm Rex Hunt and you're not.'

In one sentence he's complimenting everyone in the world bar one.

★ Two hunters got lost in the forest, so according to rescue instructions, they fired three times in the air.

But no rescue party tuned up, so they did it again and again, with no rescue party.

Finally, one hunter said, 'What are we going to do now?'

And the second hunter said, 'What can we do? We've got no more arrows left.'

★ Lorry and Bluey go on holidays and are hunting in the Canadian woods.

At night in the cabin, the alcohol is flowing and Lorry says, 'I bet you $100 I can go into the woods even at this time of night and bring back a bear skin.'

And Bluey, who was in no state to stop him, agrees to the bet. Three hours later there's a knock on the cabin door. Bluey opens the door, and standing there is an eight-foot bear.

The bear says, 'Your name Bluey?'

'Yeah', mumbles Bluey, too frightened to speak.

And the bear says, 'You know a bloke named Lorry?'

'Yeah I do.'

'Well, he owes you $100,' says the bear.

★ He's going through the woods shooting poultry, and he sees a beautiful naked girl who gives him the eye.

He says, 'Are you game?'

She says, 'Yes.'

So he shot her.

★ 'The bear chased me through the woods, and he was just inches away when I saw a tree and jumped for the branch.'

'Did you make it?'

'No,' said the hunter, 'not going up, but I caught it coming down.'

★ They made a mistake and brought a bitch beagle on heat to the fox hunt. After twenty minutes the fox was running fifth.

★ 'I just returned from a duck shoot.'

'How was it?'

'Terrible. The others shot and I had to duck.'

★ Then there is the big game hunter who has been missing now for two weeks. It is believed that something he disagreed with ate him.

★ He was a smart duck—he always flew upside-down. So if a hunter shot him, he'd fall up.

★ Wasn't it a clever man who described fox hunting, as 'the unspeakable in pursuit of the uneatable'?

★ I come from a family of air pioneers.

My father was the first to jump 3000 feet from a

plane. My brother and sister were the first to jump 8000 feet from a plane, all without parachutes. And tomorrow I'm going to jump 10,000 feet from a plane, and why not . . . I've got nothing to live for . . . I've got no family.

Olympic Sports

★We can't all be winners—
somebody has to sit on the
kerb and clap as they go by.

—Mark Twain

★ 'My brother did the 100 m and got a gold medal.'

'That's nothing—my brother did 4 m and got 6 months.'

★ 'He ran the 100 m in 6.4 seconds.'

'Ridiculous—nobody could run the 100 m in 6.4 seconds.'

'Well, he can—he knows a short-cut.'

★ Yiannis Kouros, the great long-distance runner who won the Sydney to Melbourne race, was claimed by the Greeks as one of their own, but that is unlikely.

If he was a real Greek he wouldn't have been running . . . he would have been driving a taxi.

★ The good news is, you've just been picked for the Olympic javelin team.

The bad news is, you're the one who catches it.

★ Have you heard about the Australian national cycling haircut? It's parted down the middle.

★ My brother took up karate just so he could put his fist through a block of concrete.

Should come in very handy if he's ever attacked by a cement truck.

★ She didn't know a thing about archery, but she could make her boyfriend quiver.

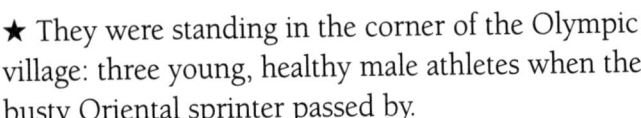

★ They were standing in the corner of the Olympic village: three young, healthy male athletes when the busty Oriental sprinter passed by.

'By Joe,' said the Englishman.

'By the beard of Allah,' said the Arab.

'By tomorrow night,' said the Australian.

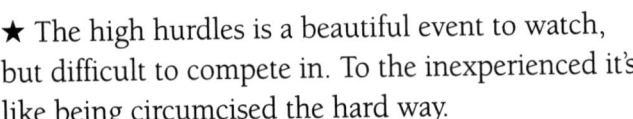

★ The high hurdles is a beautiful event to watch, but difficult to compete in. To the inexperienced it's like being circumcised the hard way.

★ It was a small country in the Olympic games—they only had one competitor and he went in for every event.

He did very well too, until he got to the relay.

He passed the baton and got disqualified for making an obscene gesture.

★ 'Yes', said the elderly lady, 'I have nine children: seven alive and two on the Olympic committee.'

★ 'I was the hop, step and jump champion but now I'm concentrating on the broad jump. Every day I practise for four hours.'

'Doesn't it get monotonous?'

'No, I practise with real broads.'

★ I believe the Olympic Committee should ban all drugs, and that includes motivational speakers.

★ The unluckiest athlete in the world: he led from start to finish in the Olympic marathon, but he didn't get a medal because it was a false start.

★ He did the 1500 m in 2 minutes 49 seconds . . . he fell over a cliff.

★ Then there was Mick. He won the Tour de France, and set off on a lap of honour.

We didn't see him for a month.

★ Ray Warren, the great League caller from Channel 9 once described the worst sportsperson he'd ever interviewed.

He said, 'If you weren't talking about him, he wasn't listening and even worse, if he wasn't listening, he wasn't talking.'

That was probably the same sportsperson who, after a flash of lightning said, 'Please, no photographs.'

★ I love the winter Olympics . . . bobsleighing fascinates me.

If it wasn't for the bobsleigh, those four people would be arrested.

★ He was faster than an Irish postman delivering a parcel to the English Embassy.

★ The secret of 74-year-old marathon runner Clif Young's success is that he's connected to iron man Guy Leach by jumper leads.

★ How can you trust China? Over a billion people and they say their favourite sport is table tennis.

★ It was the Grand Final at the shooting range, and he was favourite. But as it turned out, he gave the worst performance of his life and missed on every shot. In disgust, he turned to his team-mate at the end and said, 'I feel like shooting myself.'

And his team-mate said, 'Better take two bullets.'

★ There was once a cross-eyed javelin thrower at the Olympics. He didn't win any medals but he sure kept the crowd on their toes.

★ It was during the Cold War. The Berlin Wall was still up.

While training at night, with one jump, the East German pole-vaulting champion became the West German pole-vaulting champion.

★ Mothers can be so proud, and this pride makes them so blind.

A mother watching the fours says, 'No wonder we are not winning . . . those other three are not rowing as fast as my son!'

★ Two rowers went to Denmark for sex change operations and won Olympic gold in the coxless pairs.

★ I tell you what I think of skiing—a good pair of skis is one that converts into a pair of splints.

★ Yachting is a sport that can make you a millionaire, as long as you start off a billionaire.

★ And then there was the transvestite yachtsman, who went down to the sea in slips.

★ How is this for a bad pun: 'the boat show had a yacht to offer'.

★ Mark Spitz is all wet.

★ 'Don't criticise our squad. Every member of this swimming squad was hand-picked.'

'Well, next time,' he said, 'wait until they're ripe.'

★ The 1990 Commonwealth Games in Auckland were for me a bit like being a young toddler in a brand new sandpit and not knowing which corner to get stuck into first.

I got right into it early on with a visit to the Henderson pool which was expected to be the scene of a lot of Aussie gold. In fact some of the best highlights for me of the whole games happened on the opening morning of competition after I arrived excitedly at where the very first event of the games were to be held.

The second event of the morning featured Lisa Curry in the 100 m freestyle and she broke the Games record! There were hundreds of boxing kangaroo flags flapping, with a sprinkling of 'C'mon Aussie' banners and plenty of green and gold . . . the Aussies were there in strength and that put the pressure on accommodation that only held about 3000.

The supporters were really in what was a makeshift tin shed. However this less than beautiful structure housed a high tech swimming pool with a movable floor and end system to enable it to be broken up for other sports.

Lisa was great. She had smashed the Commonwealth Games record . . . showing that despite being a mum, the same desire and fitness

would again make her a winner. She absolutely
blitzed her competition over two laps, clocking
56.84 seconds.

That sure was a highlight, but what really took
my attention was the next event—the men's 100
metre breaststroke heat. Listed to compete were
swimmers from three very different countries . . .
Swaziland, Guernsey and Papua New Guinea.
Swaziland? This was a tiny nation in southern Africa
that doesn't even have any beaches!

Unfortunately two of the entrants failed to make
it to the pool on time . . . the young swimmers from
Swaziland and Guernsey were nowhere to be seen
or heard. No letter, phone call or message. Maybe
their flexi-fares had been converted into full price
fares during the Australian airline dispute at that
time and perhaps they couldn't afford the extra. Or
perhaps they didn't make all the complicated plane
connections or ran into financial difficulties. We'll
never know.

The lonely, remaining competitor was a kid
named Felipe Sialis from Papua New Guinea.

I remember it well from being flashed up onto the huge electronic screen at one end of the enormous swimming 'shed' in thousands of light globes. It was the only name there was . . . talk about having your name up in lights!

This was Felipe's big day and he wasn't going to miss a chance to swim in the Commonwealth Games for anything . . . he was oblivious of any opposition anyway. This was the realisation of a boyhood dream.

'You have won the heat by default,' the officials told him and they had to ask the obvious question, 'Do you still want to swim?'

This young fella was a competitor through and through . . . he hadn't trained his heart out for years and travelled—in his eyes—half way around the world not to swim. Obviously the boy Felipe from PNG said, 'YES!'

The 'race' was on. His name came across the PA and echoed around the emptiness above the 3000 seats prior to those of the two non-starters.

Channel Nine's commentators for every swimming event were the doyen of dulcet tones and international games veteran, Norman May, together with Sydney-based rugby league and horse race caller Ray 'Rabbit' Warren.

As the eight officials lined up at their various points of observation at one end of the 50 metre pool, away from the starting boxes, Ray and 'Nugget' May cast an exploratory eye over the sole swimmer's profile page: name, age, birthplace, date, nationality and career best time. No problem, now check out his background . . . the bottom two-thirds of the A4 sheet was blank!

'Nugget' and Ray Warren were sharing their three operating eyes scanning for more information about the kid from Papua New Guinea. Neither man had ever called a race with just one competitor in it. Needless to say, the information available on the kid from PNG was scant—and I bet my boots that neither of our men at the mikes had done much research on swimmers from that part of the world.

And neither had ever called a race of any kind with only one participant. Ray may have called horse races with two or three but just one was ridiculous!!!

As the starter's gun punctured the air (what a waste of a bullet!) both were well aware that the swimmer in the pool was going to take about 20 seconds longer than world record holder Adrian Morehouse to complete the two laps and that meant more air time to fill!

They were a bit nonplussed, both men had never been known to be short of a word . . . although not always the appropriate ones. I recall a classic comment from Ray a few days later when he was calling Glen Houseman in full flight . . . 'He's a swimmer!' Another time he said, 'He uses every available inch of time.'

Norman and Ray were going to exhaust all their best lines as Felipe took the limelight. Felipe hit the water like it was a big final—a mighty roar from a crowd who appreciated Felipe having a go! The clear blue water, reflecting the colour from the tiles below, was now the domain of the young man from north of Cape York. By the time his head had bobbed up and down a couple of times in the water, sucking in the air and dragging himself along, the geometric waves were rebounding off the edges of the pool.

All of a sudden the crowd became totally pre-occupied with the lone breastroker, cheering and roaring for the brown-skinned boy who knew in his heart he would not qualify for the final even after a victorious swim in the heat. The New Zealanders in the galleries enjoyed the chance to barrack for a competitor without getting drowned out by shouts of 'C'mon Aussie C'mon!'

There was a rumour doing the rounds that this was the first time the swimmer had experienced the joy of swimming in a 50 metre international standard pool!

It was said that back home he trained in the river—making sure not to cause too many ripples as they would disturb the crocodiles that floated on the surface asleep in the sun. The 'understanding' on the river was that the far bank belonged to the scaly monsters and the closest water edge was human territory . . . and provided each stayed in their own muddy water, no-one would end up a victim. At last count the score was: HUMANS eaten 7, CROCODILES eaten Nil. In theory it worked, but in reality it depended on how hungry the crocodiles were and how desperate the swimmers were to train.

Ray and Norm chose their words carefully as usual, not wasting breath or adjective but there is a limited amount to what you can talk about in a one-horse race . . . and there was still a long way to go with the end of the first 50 coming up. How do you pump up the excitement in this case? Do a 'Richie Benaud'—remain silent and let the crowd reaction tell the story?

It wasn't the finest tumbleturn we were to see in the pool but at least his fuzzy black curls were pointed in the direction of the finishing end of the pool. His split was only about 42 seconds but for Felipe the time was 'quickish'. He was now basically competing against himself, for his self-esteem and for the people who had helped him gain selection.

No need to look under an arm or over a shoulder, Felipe had his race absolutely shot to pieces . . . Ray and Norman knew it too—their call increased by about 25 decibels!

The touch of a hand against the pressure plate on the wall of the pool stopped the clock at 1:14.43—a career best swim by our 'neighbour'. He'd cut four seconds off his PB time. (About 14 seconds outside the world record.)

The kid dashed straight for the victory dais, hopped up on the gold medal spot, and thrusted the hand in the air in recognition of victory—I mean it was only a heat, he wasn't even going to get a medal! But then it was a career best time and so far he was unbeaten in the games!

Adrian Morehouse may have gone on to take the gold in this event but this fellow epitomised what sport in the purest format is all about . . . better yourself first and then if you reach the dizzy heights of being a world or Olympic champion, well and good.

This was also what the so-called friendly games was all about. One felt for this guy in this his one big moment in international sport.

Felipe's effort proved that the major battle is between the ears and within the inner body. The amount of success experienced is up to the individual. Felipe was on the way! You were memorable, mate!

★ After his first crossing of the channel, Des Renford emerged from the water and the first thing he asked for was a cup of coffee.

'Certainly Des. Milk and sugar?'

'Doesn't matter,' he said. 'I'm pouring it over my feet.'

★ I believe when Mr Renford dies, as a tribute to him his funeral procession will pass through a car wash.

★ He gave a superb display of high diving. He performed the extremely difficult side-roll reverse jack knife finish with a perfectly executed one and a half turn. Unfortunately he couldn't swim and drowned.

★ He went door to door collecting for a new swimming pool for the town. By the first day he had collected over 100 gallons of water.

★ He was doing very well in the triathlon, until he got out of the water, jumped on his bike and found out somebody had stolen the saddle.

★ He was an honest kid. He got out of the swimming pool and handed the attendant a penny.

★ My good friend Des Renford swam the English Channel nineteen times. He was going to try it one more time, but he found out they had a ferry service.

★ 'Life is a bitch', said the deep-sea diver who, coming up, passed his rescue ship going down.

★ Not many people know this.

Mick Jagger was once a life guard at Bondi Beach. He was the only one who could give the kiss of life to four people at the same time.

★ Gymnasts are starting younger and younger—in many cases, too young. And strict diet is becoming a major part of their routine. I know one coach who continually feeds his gymnasts iron pills.

It didn't make them any stronger, but they are the only kids I know who have nappy rust.

★ I like the gym teacher who told her students, 'OK. Now line up alphabetically, according to height.'

★ The karate expert rolled down the car window to signal a left-hand turn, and chopped a Volkswagen in half.

★ My younger brother took up karate just so he could put his fist through a block of concrete. It should come in very handy if he's attacked by a cement truck.

★ Before any television pictures could be beamed into households around the country for the 14th Commonwealth Games, tests needed to be undertaken. Channel Nine's central hosts—Ray Martin, Ken Sutcliffe, Mark Warren and myself were fine-tuning our performances. Every host, commentator and expert comments person, not to mention the technical back-up, had to undergo 'ON AIR' procedure.

Maybe it was a warning of trials to come when we crossed to the weightlifting for a chat with Darrell Eastlake. A couple of the Aussie lifters were working out, so we asked 'Decibel Dazza' to wind up and give us a sample of things to come. Well, Big Daz unleashed a 30-odd second tirade of high-pitched, 40 decibel-plus screaming . . .

He was describing Gregory Hayman in the 52 kg class . . . 'On goes the resin . . . a dust of the hands . . . look at him spread those fingers . . . now he sucks it in . . . a 'HUGE' breath . . . wraps the fingers around . . . and look at him go . . . those driving muscles in those 'HUGE' thighs . . . vibrating, vibrating . . . now he steadies for the jerk . . . look at the strain . . . veins bulging . . . cheeks full blown . . . he's gonna do it . . . yes, green 'n' gold . . . wow, what a lift . . . 'HUUUUUGGGGGE! In fact, a new Commonwealth record—well done Greg Hayman!'

'Now look at that Dean . . . that's really put the pressure on the Indians?'

With that his quieter spoken apprentice, 'LA' Olympic gold medallist, Dean Lukin, set about emulating big Dazza's call!

Fine for sound . . . but could we hear the call without the sound volume turned up on our sets? Thanks. Picture perfect. Only a piece of laminex-covered particleboard half a metre high and the width of the desk separated the British caller from Darrell and Dean on one side and the New Zealand commentating team to the right. Straight ahead, beyond the 60 cm wide desk top was clear vision of the performance—absolutely no sound-proofing or acoustic treatment at all.

So after the booming dress rehearsal by Darrell, Dean and former Australian Coach, Mike Noonan, one caller seated three desk tops away to the right promptly slammed close his briefcase and stormed out muttering something about not being able to operate under such a ridiculous handicap.

That wasn't Channel Nine's problem . . . and no more thought was given to it! We were all set at the weightlifting, well that was until the competition got underway . . .

Dean was by now enjoying being under the tutorage of 'Whispering Jack' Eastlake and as the days wore on, the tuna fisherman from Port Lincoln in South Australia, and one of weightlifting's more serene big men, kept getting louder and louder—even at the bar!

When they started off commentating on Day One from the public seating area of the auditorium, they were soon shouting the praises of the son of a Tasmanian shearer, Ronny Laycock, after he hoisted Australia's first two gold medals by taking out the clean 'n' jerk and snatch in the 75 kg division.

Despite that great start, the Australians were doomed to relinquish the teams trophy for the first time in 12 years.

Darrell who began talking . . . then as usual gets excited as he has always done from a beginning of a career path during the late 60s doing pioneering surf reports for radio 2UW in Sydney, was about to become the victim of bureaucratic interference.

The man who unashamedly has left an indelible mark and sound on the sport of weightlifting in Australia apparently upset one important member of the audience—the New Zealand Governor-General, Sir Paul Reeves!

The rumour was that the regal gent complained bitterly that an Australian commentator was upsetting his degree of comfort with his booming voice. It could only be Darrell, who 'hates' getting excited!

Consequently Sir Paul ordered him removed and so he was . . . gee, they operate like sheep over there—one moves or goes 'Baah Bah' and the others follow. Isn't the land of the long grey cloud the place where men aren't necessarily men and the sheep are very nervous? Or was it to do with the density of sheep per acre and the exceptionally high sales of gum boots? Luckily I can't remember.

Silence has never been one of Dazza's hobbies and he reckoned it was 'a bloody joke!'

'It's unbelievable and I suspect they didn't want

Prince Edward (who attended the weightlifting the next day) to cop an earful!'

The big problem remained—how do they and we solve the situation and ensure that the weightlifting coverage not lose out? Simple! Lock 'em in a soundproof cupboard.

★ As the weight-lifter said when he looked down at the room full of coaches, 'It's not the ups and downs that bother me, it's the jerks.'

★ When the great scorer comes to write against your name, he marks not that you have won or lost, but how you've played the game.

—*Garland Rice*